Praise for *Rituals for Virtual Meetings*

"Kursat and Glenn offer useful insights about our everyday interactions, and they turned those insights into practical tools. This is a handbook for anyone who has ever wanted to transform a virtual meeting from an exhausting slog into an energizing and enjoyable playground."

—Emi Kolawole, General Troublemaker & Head of Internal Communications at X The Moonshot Factory

"Workplace rituals are a powerful, unspoken tool to build community, strengthen culture, and enhance belonging—whether you're in person or in a virtual work space. Kursat and Glenn's compelling compendium is a roll-up-your-sleeves deep dive into innovative, business-savvy ritual design that will help you and your co-workers purposefully, meaningfully, and creatively gather together online."

—Annette Ferrara, Workplace Experience Director, IDEO

"For centuries, humans have innately understood that small, tangible acts done routinely can carry value and meaning. These "rituals" can help build the muscle memory of an organization's culture. I am excited that this book helps now more humans to leverage the power of rituals and bring them to life in new ways, preparing organizations for a new virtual normal. The authors offer guidance on how to experiment with rituals in virtual meetings, taking an organization's culture ultimately from good to great."

—Dr. Frederik G. Pferdt, Google's Chief Innovation Evangelist; Adjunct Professor, Stanford University

Rituals for Virtual Meetings

Creative Ways to Engage People
and Strengthen Relationships

Kürşat Özenç, PhD
Glenn Fajardo

WILEY

For general information on our other products and services or for technical support, please contact our Customer Care Department within the United States at (800) 762-2974, outside the United States at (317) 572-3993 or fax (317) 572-4002.
Wiley publishes in a variety of print and electronic formats and by print-on-demand. Some material included with standard print versions of this book may not be included in e-books or in print-on-demand. If this book refers to media such as a CD or DVD that is not included in the version you pur-chased, you may download this material at http://booksupport.wiley.com. For more information about Wiley products, visit www.wiley.com.
Library of Congress Cataloging-in-Publication Data is available:
ISBN 9781119755999 (paperback)
ISBN 9781119755982 (ePDF)
ISBN 9781119756019 (ePub)
Cover Design and Illustration: Kürsat Özenç
10 9 8 7 6 5 4 3 2 1

Kürşat dedicates this book to Margaret, Kerem, Teoman, and Leyla.

Glenn dedicates this book to Mom and Dad.

Contents

PART THREE
Beyond the "Office"

Ritual Index

Profiles

Jeff Zacks 53

Associate Chair, Department of Psychological and Brain Sciences; Professor of Psychological and Brain Sciences; Professor of Radiology

Nick Fortugno 37

Game Designer and Educator at Parsons; CCO of Playmatics

J. P. Stephens 117

Associate Professor of Organizational Behavior at Case Western Reserve University - Weatherhead School of Management

Marica Rizzo 86

Community Manager, Acumen

Laila von Alvensleben 148

Head of Culture and Collaboration at MURAL

Jane Dutton 178

Professor at University of Michigan (Emerita)

Jesper Frøkjær Sørensen 209

Associate Professor, Department of the Study of Religion, Aarhus University

Joumana Mattar 240

Service and Organizational Change Manager at 4AM | An EY Venture

Leticia Britos Cavagnaro 274

Co-Director, University Innovation Fellows Program and Adjunct Professor, d.school, Stanford University

Mario Roset 305

Co-Founder and CEO at Civic House

OUR BOOK TEAM
FAREWELL RITUAL

Hello!

How Rituals Make Virtual Meetings More Engaging, Productive, and Meaningful

1

The Power of Rituals in Transforming Virtual Meetings

Introduction

"Imagine if tomorrow — like literally tomorrow, the day after today — there was some kind of global disaster, and suddenly humans could interact only through computers. It's unclear when — or if — face-to-face contact will be possible again. It might be a while. Maybe that disaster is a zombie apocalypse, or a sudden change in the atmosphere, or something else."

This is a prompt for an exercise called "Virtual Humanity" that one of us (Glenn) developed in 2017. We never imagined this exercise would become too real in early 2020. People were scrambling to make virtual "work" in schools, businesses, nonprofits, governments, and communities. Virtual collaboration had previously been an emerging topic in "future of work" discussions, but suddenly became a pressing topic in "present of work" conversations. People were suddenly struggling to connect.

Humans are social beings. We are wired to connect with other people to feel alive and well (Liebermann, 2013). Without connection, our very existence is in danger and crisis. In the COVID-19 pandemic of 2020, we found ourselves in the midst of such a crisis across all walks of life. Social distancing made "social" feel distant.

In theory, we had a set of miracle technologies that could help us stay connected. When you think about it, it's kind of crazy that technology such as video conferencing – or the Internet itself – could be so widely available. But in reality, it was frustrating for many people. Why?

Part of it was the limitations of the technology. For example, there were many news articles about difficulties on Zoom calls, with common themes such as Zoom not accounting for things such as cues, synchrony and mimicry (how humans synchronize and mimic each other), eye contact, who's where in the grid, and constantly seeing yourself.

However, there was a more fundamental problem. *Many of the norms and conventions from in-person meetings didn't work well in the virtual meetings that we were suddenly thrown into.*

People largely tried to recreate what they did in-person in their virtual meetings, largely because that's the only experience that was familiar to them. Many people approached virtual meetings with a deficit mindset where "it's never as good as in-person," and they ended up with sad, second-rate copies of in-person experiences. So the screen-bound interactions frustrated people (Murphy, 2020), made them feel awkward, and tired them out (Kost, 2020). People longed for better human connection.

However, if we are honest with ourselves, we weren't thriving at connecting and building relationships in-person before the COVID-19 pandemic forced people completely online.

The so-called loneliness epidemic had been sweeping the world. By 2020, three out of five Americans were feeling lonely and a sense of abandonment (Renken, 2020). The U.K. government, for instance, assigned a minister to address the challenges of loneliness (Yeginsu, 2018). By 2015, China was raising the "loneliest generation" as the one-child policy was just ending (Wong, 2019). Loneliness is related to higher health risk and premature death (Holt-Lunstad, 2018).

Work life has been reinforcing this feeling of isolation with its sterile workplace conditions and its culture. Engagement across the U.S. workforce has been fluctuating around 30% for the past two decades (Adkins, 2016). The disengagement and a sense of loneliness increases when coworkers don't have shared goals. Meetings are one of the most prominent manifestations of lack of common purpose. 67% of meetings are seen as failures (Gandhi, 2019). Meetings are perceived both as a necessity and a curse. On the one hand, they can be key to moving things forward. But on the other hand, they often end up as missed opportunities to connect and as distractions to deep work.

We believe meetings are moments to be elevated and nurtured.

Good meetings help people build relationships, align on purpose, and get things done, whether a meeting is in-person or virtual. However, virtual is newer terrain for most people. The challenge is the disorienting unfamiliarity. The opportunity is the possibility to have deeper connections, shared purpose, and greater accomplishments wherever we are.

Rituals can support us with scaffolding as we find our footing in virtual meetings.

Our perspective is informed by our experiences in virtual collaboration and ritual design, including both of our teaching experiences at the d.school, a.k.a. the Hasso Plattner Institute of Design, at Stanford University. For 12 years, Glenn has been a practitioner of virtual collaboration, working with people and organizations across six continents engaged in social impact work. He specializes in teaching classes and workshops on how to collaborate virtually, such

as Design Across Borders. Kursat has been teaching and researching rituals with students and partner organizations both in the U.S. and in Europe. He shared his recent learnings from his teaching and consulting in *Rituals for Work* (Ozenc, 2019).

Our perspective is rooted in a vision that virtual meetings can be satisfying experiences with high-intensity and high-quality human connection, like a good movie. The inspiration for this vision comes from an unusual place: Sufi concepts of time and space. Kursat grew up in a culture where mythical Sufi stories shape the hustle and bustle of everyday life.

Bast-i zaman and Tayyi-mekan

In Sufism, the concept of *bast-i zaman* articulates the possibility **of expanding time within a set time.** A surprising number of important things can happen in a short amount of time when there's alignment between the individual(s) and a higher purpose. For instance, you can finish a month-long task in an hour when you experience this alignment and connection.

In organizational psychology research, Jane Dutton talks about a similar idea with her high-quality connections concept. She defines a high-quality connection as a "shorter-term interaction you have with someone virtually or face-to-face, in which both people feel lit up and energized by the connection." Jane articulates how to nurture such a rich relationship with empathy, resilience, and openness.

The concept of *tayyi-mekan* adds another layer to the high-quality connections. If a Sufi passes certain spiritual states of consciousness, there is a sense in which he can be **present in multiple places at once**. It's somewhat analogous to a person being virtually present to colleagues in different parts of the world. But the concept is deeper than that. You might have noticed that there's a difference between simply appearing on a screen in a virtual meeting and feeling present to your colleagues. In Sufism, multiple presences happen when people feel a core presence of a shared goal and purpose (i.e. unity with a higher cause). Virtual meetings are most engaging when participants feel a strong sense of shared purpose, and rituals can help. There's a strong body of ritual know-how that is rooted in centuries-old traditions of connection and community, from Sufism to Zen Buddhism. More principles from such traditions are waiting to be rediscovered as ways to guide virtual connection and community.

How do we make this vision of core presence and connection a reality? We draw upon three inspirational spaces: 1) waves of experimentation during the pandemic, 2) audiovisual arts and game design, 3) cognitive science and organizational psychology.

During the COVID-19 pandemic, preventive measures such as shelter-in-place forced people to connect with other people virtually, and the world felt like a big laboratory of social interactions. From virtual whiteboard games (Alvensleben, 2018) to sing-a-long rituals of Italian neighborhoods (Kearney, 2020), these experiments created energy to define new ways of interacting and participating. We think experimentation can be further sharpened with the tools of design thinking, where we notice underlying needs, define actionable opportunities, and experiment rapidly.

We're inspired by what we can draw from audiovisual arts and game design. There's a lot we can learn from how movies, radio shows, and games create alternate worlds that we can enter, engage in, and come out changed.

For example, consider screen fatigue. How often do you get screen fatigue when watching movies or Netflix? It's probably a lot less often than you do with video conference meetings. But why? Some of it has to do with the level of concentration required, but some of it has to do with how movies are in some ways closer to how we see the world. (We'll explain that and other inspirations in Chapter 3.) This book will help you plan your meetings with a narrative structure so they feel a little more exciting and memorable, a little more like a movie.

This book will also draw on cognitive science and organizational psychology. These fields have critical insights that help us interact in more human ways when we are not in the same room. When we understand a bit more about how our brain works and how groups work, we can create meetings that feel more human using technologies available today. Helping you do that in your virtual meetings is the goal of this book.

Challenges of Virtual Meetings

If we reflect on our relationships, we would discover that meetings – in the broader sense of the term – are the cornerstone of our work and social lives. From two-person coffee chats to gatherings of thousands of people, we meet to talk, explore, and do things together. When we shift from in-person meetings to virtual, we observe the following challenges.

Our use of our senses changes

During a physical experience, such as an annual retreat party with our colleagues, we use all our senses. People without disabilities can see, hear, smell, touch, and taste. The music we hear, the food we eat, and the friends we see at that party can combine to create special moments. Research shows that we use our senses in pairs. For instance, vision and sound complement each other to increase our understanding of space.

How we use our senses changes dramatically with the way most virtual meetings are run today. There's an overload to hearing and seeing – and an underload to touching, smelling and tasting – which can lead to getting burned out. Without the engagement of a broader array of senses, we have less fulfilling experiences. To have more fulfilling virtual experiences, we need to learn how we can engage our different senses together when we are not in the same place.

Tech is not quite there yet

Katie is a senior manager at a medium-sized company. She leads a team of six people while being part of multiple cross-functional initiatives with her peers in the company. She spends her days on back-to-back virtual meetings in front of a laptop across multiple time zones. She feels drained after work, making it hard to connect with her family.

Research shows that when people are using video conferencing during virtual meetings, they experience a different cognitive load. As psychiatrist Emily Williams described, with videoconferencing, we both have too much and too little. We have too much of the illusion of presence and too little of the information that comes with physical presence (Petriglieri, 2020). There can be slight delays that throw you off. We're not sure how long to look, where to look, and when to do so. If you stared at people's faces too much with videoconferencing in 2020, you'd experience this dissonance in a way that forced you to expend extra effort and energy. And so Katie gets drained.

Social expectations are unclear

The year 2020 will partly be remembered as the year of awkward virtual social gatherings.

Larry lives with his daughter and wife. They attended 10 virtual social gatherings together in a month. The ambiguity during those well-intentioned gatherings became wearisome, with countless awkward moments when people didn't know what to say to whom.

When we get together for the sake of a project in a work context, we at least have some sense of direction since there's a shared goal of completing something. When we get together virtually for strictly social reasons, it can be hard to deeply connect with people. Up to this point in history, the intimacy that we feel with most of our friends and family has been mediated by the spatial relationship between our bodies. When we suddenly could not be in the same physical spaces, we didn't understand how to sustain connections. In unfamiliar virtual terrain and without a clear purpose for social gatherings, we didn't know what to do when we were together. And it was socially awkward to leave.

Unfamiliar context disorients

The previous three challenges all contribute to a broader challenge: The context of virtual can be disorienting because it is unfamiliar and so different from what we are used to in-person.

Let's illustrate this with an analogy. Imagine you were suddenly thrown into space on a spacecraft. (Let's imagine you had a pressurized cabin with oxygen which kept you alive.) Gravity works differently. You start moving in three dimensions instead of two, and moving around feels completely different. You experience touch differently because your feet aren't grounded. (There is no "ground!")

If you were a trained astronaut, you'd be totally fine. If anything, you'd be exhilarated because you were prepared for the context so you could navigate it and enjoy it. But if you weren't prepared for the context of space, you might get anxious, frustrated, and maybe queasy.

When people suddenly go from the familiar in-person to the unfamiliar virtual, it's like going from Earth to space.

When we meet physically, we know how to go about it based on our understanding of the context. While having a conversation, that familiar physical context fills in the spaces that we do not explicitly cover. It helps us understand the situation, read the room, and steer our conversations with other people.

When we meet virtually, we can get disoriented because we're not yet used to the context. In this unfamiliar territory, we don't have the familiar norms and interaction rituals of the physical world. We don't have subtle cues such as the full body language of a person to build a context.

To summarize, virtual meetings pose several challenges. To sustain a healthy conversation with people during a meeting, we need to have an understanding of context. Many people have virtual interactions where context is not yet well-understood, and many people are not yet aware of how we can use more of our senses in virtual. Without a good footing, people put in extra effort to sustain interactions and conversations, which leads to strenuous cognitive load. Being in situations that lack clear purpose – such as many virtual social gatherings – can also cause challenges around emotional well-being.

The Power of Rituals for Virtual Meetings

When we face an unfamiliar context that disorients and challenges our well-being, we look for tangible things and experiences to hold on to (Winnicott, 1973). These tangible things and experiences give us a sense of control and order. One vivid example of this is a toddler's security blanket. When a child begins to perceive that she is a different person than her parents, she is in disarray like that non-astronaut in space. Growing into independence is exhilarating, but it's also disorienting on many different levels. Emotions are like an iceberg with some delight above water but a lot of fear and anxiety beneath the surface. The security blanket helps the child to adapt to this new state of being. Later in life, instead of a security blanket, we use and sometimes invent rituals to overcome anxiety that comes with new circumstances (Evans-Pritchard, 1965). Rituals in that sense are an evolutionary human invention, to adapt and grow into new states of being.

Rituals from the Trobriand fishermen tribe in Papua New Guinea tell us a lot about how rituals can help people in times of unfamiliarity. The tribe has two distinct fishing practices. When the fishermen fish in the safe harbor of the nearby lagoon lake, they go about their fishing routine without any ceremony. When the fishermen decide to fish in the open waters of the ocean, they deploy elaborate magic rituals to feel safe. Rituals provide them perceived control (Malinowski, 1948).

In-person meetings are our safe harbor, and virtual meetings are our open waters. Rituals can address the contextual unknowns of the virtual relationships. Rituals can mitigate the risks associated with those unknowns by emotionally and mentally preparing people.

How do rituals work and address such a fundamental need for adaptation? Rituals are complex experiences. They can operate at different scales at once. From a bird's, eye view, rituals can give form to an entire experience, such as a graduation ceremony. From a first-person view, rituals can also shape how two people interact when they first meet, such as a greeting ritual. On both scales, it helps people to adapt and live well with other people and their environment. Ritual does this by taking a mundane routine moment and flips it into something meaningful and special.

What do we mean by ritual?

In our work over the years, we've observed that people use practices, games, activities, and routines interchangeably with rituals. To clarify what we mean by ritual, we will give our working definition:

Rituals are acts that we perform with intention following a pattern. They involve a symbolism that helps us invest and harvest meaning in those special moments (Ozenc and Hagan, 2019).

The power of rituals comes from flipping mundane moments into special ones. Moments are the ingredients of rituals, as flour is for bread. The strength of rituals comes from elevating negative or dull emotions in those moments to positive emotions with energy.

Before we go further, let's make a clear distinction between a routine and a *ritual*. Rituals have *routine* qualities in that they are repetitive and require you to follow a pattern. However, unlike routines, rituals are conscious and *intentional*. A routine is unconscious and unremarkable. A ritual is mindful and memorable. When rituals lose their intention, they decay into routines that hold less meaning.

Let's illustrate with a simple example, the "How are you?" greeting at the beginning of a meeting. If people respond in a reflexive, "Fine, how are you?" regardless of how they are really doing, that's more like a routine. If people intentionally share how they are really feeling, that's closer to a ritual of checking in with each other.

Rituals have five qualities that can help turn mundane virtual meetings to meaningful experiences:

1. Rituals can help us clarify, reinforce, and renew purpose.

Have you ever been to a meeting where it wasn't clear why you were meeting, where there wasn't a clear purpose? This is extra awkward in virtual meetings! Why?

Most people are still figuring out how to read intentions and convey intentions in the context of a virtual meeting. When the purpose of a meeting is unclear and people's intentions are unclear, the ingredients for commonality are missing. A ritual can help a group articulate a purpose – why group members are meeting – by making intentions explicit with ritual actions and words.

Rituals can also connect the ritual participants, mentally and emotionally. Research on *high-quality connections* by University of Michigan professor Jane Dutton and her collaborators shows how connecting with people is a critical aspect of teamwork. When we have high-quality connections with other people, we feel positive regard, mutuality, and vitality. Positive regard is the sense that someone sees the best in us. Mutuality means we feel a sense of responsiveness and openness from another person. Vitality is the energy we feel when deeply connected to someone else (Dutton, Heaphy, 2016).

If we do not form these relational connections, it's more difficult to get things done as a group. When people connect, they can internalize the group's intention as their own, and move together toward the purpose gracefully.

2. Rituals can bring order by giving shape to virtual experiences.

The other big challenge we articulated earlier is the cognitive overload many of us experience when we virtually meet. We need to spend more mental and emotional energy when in unfamiliar and disorienting terrain. One way to reduce cognitive load is to shape virtual meetings well so people use less mental power. Rituals are designed experiences that give form and structure.

What might be that form and structure? Artistic experiences can give us a clue, such as the three-act structure for many Hollywood movies. Whether we are talking about *Star Wars* or *When Harry Met Sally*, there's setup, confrontation and resolution (Field, Syd. 1994). That structure helps give a shape to that movie. (We'll talk more about what we can learn from movies in Chapter 3.)

Similarly, a well-crafted meeting has different sections that give it shape, along with transitions to connect the pieces together. There are ritual moments that can mark these stages of the experience, and these markers can help navigate the less familiar terrain of virtual meetings.

Many of the rituals in this book can help you shape your virtual meetings.

3. Rituals can visualize our desired states/goals.

When we are in unfamiliar territory, we rely on our imagination to fill in the gaps in our understanding. Barbara Tversky calls this one of the laws of cognition: The mind fills in missing information. For instance, you might be having a hard time reading where people are, mentally and emotionally, during a virtual meeting. Your mind fills that gap based on your past experiences, and it may or may not be terribly accurate.

Alternatively, rituals can help team members to fill that gap together by activating people's imaginations with symbols and symbolic acts. Rituals help us visualize the desired state for that situation. In ritualistic moments, we suspend reality to get closer to the desired state we yearn for. As Clifford Geertz said, "in a ritual, the world as lived and the world as imagined … turn out to be the same world" (Geertz, 1973). The Olympic Workout ritual in Chapter 6 for instance brings the symbolism around super athletes. By picking Serena Williams, the participant enters an imagined space where she can be a Serena Williams for several minutes by performing a micro-workout. In this ritual, the suspension of reality helps the participant to act out a super athlete role.

Let's illustrate the imaginative power of ritual with one from the Bororo tribe in Brazil. Bororo tribes live in the Amazon, and macaw parrots are an important part of their culture. These birds are representatives of gods and ancestors. The tribe has a coming-of-age ritual where young men wear feathers of macaws and perform a dance to become one of the adult men. By identifying themselves with the macaws, they become one of the Bororo men. By wearing their feathers, they fly like the souls of their ancestors. Everyday life is transformed into a sacred moment for these young men (Turner, 1991).

In a classroom setting, you can create a tangible symbol to support the learning objectives of your class. At work, new employees can benefit from team-specific symbols to familiarize themselves with the team culture and become part of a team as they internalize the team symbol.

4. Rituals can create a healthy rhythm in virtual meetings with clear cues, gestures, and phrases.

When we are together in the same physical space in a ritual, we can read people's faces and body gestures to understand and respond to them. We know when to take turns, when to listen.

We know from neuroscience that people mirror each other to empathize with each other and synchronize with each other (Tversky, 2019). There's a rhythm to these interactions. If the rhythm is off, people will feel off.

In virtual meetings, we're less confident in developing the rhythm of interactions because we don't yet have clear cues. For example, have you ever been in a video meeting and had trouble getting a sense of when another person is about to stop talking? "Um, is it my turn now, or are you about to say more?"

Rituals can reduce awkwardness by creating clear turn-taking cues, using gestures and phrases. To better design these gestures and phrases, we can borrow from the work of Erving Goffman, one of most influential sociologists of the twentieth century.

Goffman described our interactions as a pattern with three steps: 1) *Initiation* (showing I am about to start a conversation), 2) *Turn taking* (continuing from where another person left off), and 3) *Leavetaking* (signalling and ending a conversation) (Goffman, 1963).

In this model, we start our interactions with others with simple rituals like a greeting ritual. After initiation, the rest is a chain of turn takings. For instance, I express a thought, signal the end of my talking, and stop.

The other person responds to me, and stops. Then, I continue from where the other person left off, and so on. We close our interactions with a leavetaking, which means signalling to the other person to end the conversation, such as a farewell gesture.

Here's an example:

Initiation
A- Hello, How are you doing?
B- Great, I am doing fine, how about you?
A- Doing alright, thank you.

Turn taking
A- I saw that you completed the section on rituals.
B- Yes, I also worked on the illustrations.
A- ....

Leavetaking
A- Alright, we covered a lot today, we are at the hour ... talk to you next week.
B- Yep, it was a great session, have a nice rest of the day.

In virtual meetings, designing cues for Goffman's interaction patterns might be relatively easy. Imagine if we had gestures and phrases that everyone understands to indicate when a person is done taking a turn and when they would like a turn to talk. For example, in the Pass the

Mic ritual (in Chapter 10), when the person talking is done with their turn, they can use a prop and a gesture. This reinforces that the person now is done with her turn.

Designing cues doesn't have to be complicated. Parents of young children do it all the time, because sometimes they don't want little Johnny to know that we're not having P-I-Z-Z-A tonight like we usually do on Tuesdays. So do young people going on double dates, because if I make the secret signal, we're going to find a way to hit eject.

5. Rituals can energize people with emotional and mental payoff moments.

When people engage in a ritual, it energizes them and elevates their well-being. Randall Collins coined the term *emotional effervescence* for this payoff quality that can emerge from a ritual (Collins, 2004). This energy can physically recharge, emotionally connect, mentally satisfy, and spiritually align people with their purpose (Vallance, 2019). Schwartz and Loehr identified these four kinds of energy (Loehr and Schwartz, 2007) that can be channeled with rituals and other intentional practices.

These payoff moments are also what makes rituals stick. For instance, Marica Rizzo told us about a meditation ritual she runs with her team to help clear their minds and prepare them for the meeting. One time, when she forgot the ritual, a couple of teammates reminded her to run the ritual. For them, the emotional payoff was strong enough to insist on the ritual. Successful rituals have this power to move people and contribute to their well-being in subtle yet effective ways.

From this point of departure to the journey ahead

By making intentions clear, giving structure to experiences, visualizing desired states, and facilitating interactions with clear cues and signals, rituals transform dull and awkward moments into meaningful and graceful moments. We will show how these principles manifest themselves in specific rituals.

This book will help you engage people and strengthen relationships in your virtual life. We will help you understand principles by showing you how they work in practical use, demonstrating with rituals from a variety of people (including us!). We'll give you some backstory on how these rituals emerged and evolved. We'll include practical suggestions for adapting them to your context. And we'll profile practitioners and experts who are leading the way to rituals for better virtual meetings.

Part 1 of this book, which includes Chapter 1, describes how rituals make virtual meetings more

engaging, productive, and meaningful. In Chapter 2, we define and articulate the elements of a meeting and how rituals can help shape those elements. We then explain six ritual keys to unlock the path for more satisfying meetings. In Chapter 3, we explore the Secret Science of Virtual Meetings, how we can make virtual more human by understanding our underlying needs and drawing from fields such as moviemaking, cognitive science, and game design.

Part 2 of the book describes various rituals for virtual meetings. In Chapter 4, we showcase rituals for opening and closing meetings. In Chapter 5, we feature rituals for focus, engagement, and flow. In Chapter 6, we address issues around Zoom fatigue, and rituals that can help individuals and teams to rejuvenate and increase resilience. In Chapter 7, we share rituals for building connections and relationships. In Chapter 8, we address challenges around 1:1 meetings. In Chapter 9, we feature rituals for transitions and shifting culture.

Part 3 of the book looks at areas beyond work. In Chapter 10, we demonstrate rituals for teaching and training. In Chapter 11, we showcase rituals for virtual social gatherings.

Think of the rituals in this book like recipes in a cookbook. When you read a cookbook, you probably don't expect to make every single dish. Instead, you look at different possibilities to see which dishes might be exciting for you and for the people you're cooking for. You may follow a recipe exactly, or you might use it more for inspiration to launch you into your own dish idea. We'll be excited to hear about the tasty meals of rituals you put together to nourish yourself and others with meaning.

As you explore the different rituals ahead, keep these key takeaways in mind:

1. Meetings are the cornerstone for human connection, getting things done, and building relationships. Meetings are good when they are done right whether they are in-person or virtual.

2. Virtual meetings are challenging, due to the lack of norms and conventions, unfamiliarity of context, and limitations in technology.

3. Rituals are a way to get to good meetings.

4. Rituals can help us clarify, reinforce, and renew purpose.

5. Rituals can bring order by giving structure to virtual experiences.

6. Rituals visualize our desired states/goals.

7. Rituals synchronize our virtual interactions by cues, gestures, and phrases.

8. Rituals energize people with emotional/mental payoff moments.

2

Meetings as Moments to Be Elevated and Nurtured

In this chapter, we will define what a meeting is and how it differs when it's in-person or virtual. We will then break down virtual meeting elements and explain how rituals can help people have a better meeting. We will then identify five ritual keys that can unlock the paths to better meetings.

What's a Meeting?

"Meeting" in the *Oxford Dictionary* is defined as the coming together of two or more people by chance or arrangement. We act, think, and sometimes feel together. Different meetings serve different purposes. Formal meetings tend to have a more explicit structure. Informal meetings tend to get their energy from our social instincts. In both, meetings help us feel connected.

IN-PERSON
POTATO

VIRTUAL
RICE

In-Person and Virtual

As a rough analogy, we can think of in-person meetings and virtual meetings like potatoes and rice. Potatoes and rice are both starches, but they have different qualities. It's not that one is good and one is bad. They can bring different things to the party in your tummy. They both can be yummy.

In an in-person meeting, things are physically situated and defined. We have a strong sense of space, of distance, and direction in three dimensions. This has profound effects on the ways in which we can perceive people and things through sight, sound, and touch. We read body language of people's full bodies.

In a virtual meeting, things are technologically mediated. We can have limitless spaces available to us. We can be together anywhere at any time, over time. For example, we could have a daily 10-minute mind-meld with a colleague on the other side of world. We can interact through multiple channels in combination. We can save, scale, and remix more easily when desired.

VIRTUAL MEETING ELEMENTS

Elements of Rituals That Can Help People Have a Better Meeting

Goal(s)
Time
Roles
Words
Gestures (Non-verbal cues)
People's Energy

SOME REASONS WHY PEOPLE WANT TO MEET

ALIGNING
EXPECTATIONS

SOLVING
PROBLEMS

IMPLEMENTING
A SOLUTION

MAKING A
DECISION

PLANNING

Goals

Meeting goals matter because we need a north star to guide our journey.

To get to specific goals, we can start by thinking about the type of meeting we are holding. For example, we might be aligning stakeholders and expectations, solving problems, making decisions, planning, implementing, or decreasing ambiguity.

We are much more likely to have a successful meeting when we make our meeting goals clear. Goals tightly couple with meeting outcomes.

Rituals can make goals tangible and explicit. Rituals can help people to articulate goals in more concrete ways. At the beginning of some rituals, goals are spelled out as intentions. For instance, in a Haka ritual before a rugby game, the goals are boosting confidence of the team and fans while inducing fear in opponents. By making goals clear, rituals can help increase our sense of control by decreasing ambiguity.

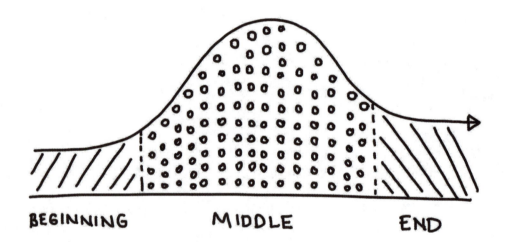

BEGINNING   MIDDLE   END

Time

"Time" here is not about what time of day your meeting takes place or how many minutes your meeting lasts. We're talking about time in a more profound sense: *How do your meeting participants experience the passage of time in your meeting?*

Do parts of the meeting feel like they take forever? Do other parts seem to whiz by before you know it?

Rituals can help people better structure time, pace the rhythm of the meeting, and manage people's energy.

You can make your meetings more effective by having clearly marked beginnings, middle sections, and endings. Rituals can mark time and make transitions more explicit. (We'll explain why this matters in Chapter 3.)

And meetings benefit from highlight moments that can make them memorable, such as a reveal of a solution for a client meeting. A 30-second reveal moment can make a 2-hour meeting feel magical.

Roles

In our social interactions, we can take on roles as a way to feel in control and show our best selves. Some roles are based on a job function, such as a manager and an individual contributor.

Some roles are based on a situation, such as being asked to be an active participant for a particular meeting. Factors such as power dynamics, personalities, and cultural backgrounds can affect people's participation.

One way to overcome these challenges is to make these situational roles more explicit and desirable. When a meeting organizer makes a role explicit and desirable, it opens up a safe space for people to perform and express themselves.

Rituals can help create and position roles in a gathering. In virtual meetings, an organizer can create roles such as storyteller and collaborator, to help people to come out of their reserved selves. The Pass the Question ritual in Chapter 10 is an example of how this can be done. The instructor helps students act like an instructor and pose open-ended questions to their peers.

Words

Words set the tone and energy of a meeting at the start. Questions, prompts, and participants' conversations carry that tone and energy during the meeting. Words affect the energy of the close of a meeting.

In priming people for the meeting goals and the meeting topic, in facilitating the conversations between meeting participants, rituals can make spoken words more interactive and amplify their effect. When someone says, "Hello, how are you doing?" flatly, without the ritual, it would feel dry. When the same person follows a greeting ritual with gestures, facial expressions, and energy, it would create a feeling of warmth on both sides.

In some gatherings, ritual turns spoken words into symbols for the group. For instance, one of our designer friends, Ayse Birsel, has a pre-meeting ritual. Before a high-stakes meeting, she gets together with her team to sing the "We Are the Champions" song together. The title of the song becomes a symbolic phrase that charges them with high energy. Its function goes from functional to symbolic to boost confidence of participants.

Gestures

We are wired to communicate with gestures as they help us better express ourselves and understand each other. As Barbara Tversky observes, "Gestures express so many meanings directly; words take time to find and to assemble" (Tversky, 2019). Gestures can be used to facilitate 1:1 interactions and also can be used to sync a group of people.

There is science and art behind gestures. Let's talk about the art first. In improv theater, one of the cornerstone activities to warm up actors and actresses is called the Mirror Game. Actors and actresses mimic each other in an improvisational way. They don't know in advance how the other person will gesture. This mirroring syncs people before the actual rehearsal. In a meeting, an organizer or facilitator could use gestures to sync and prime people for collaborative work.

Lior Noy looked at the same mirror game from a scientific perspective and found that when two people tune into each other's movements and proactively respond to the gestures in the moment, they can experience a sense of togetherness (Noy, 2014). Both of these insights are powerful and can be leveraged in crafting a meeting.

Energy

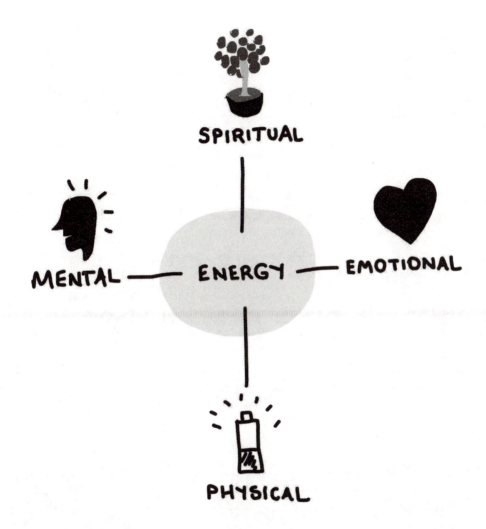

Loehr and Schwartz discovered people have four sources of energy (Schwartz and McCarthy, 2005).

People have limited energy on any given day. People allocate this energy between individual and collaborative work over the course of the day. They switch between the focus and collaboration modes. People need to adapt quickly in changing these modes. In between meetings, when their energy drains, they need to rejuvenate. Rituals can manage the energy between these different modes and contexts.

What keys do people need to focus on to unlock the paths for a good meeting?

1. Beginning and Ending a Meeting with Engagement

2. Focus, Engagement, and Flow

3. Resilience and Rejuvenation

4. Creating Connection and Building Relationships

5. Transitions and Shifting Culture Transition

A meeting organizer and participants expect to accomplish certain goals in a meeting. In order to achieve these goals, they need to consider the following keys to unlock the paths for a satisfying meeting:

1. Beginning and Ending a Meeting with Engagement

Beginnings and endings matter. In the beginnings, the meeting organizer needs to prime the participants to think and act together. This priming helps people start with the right energy level and expectations. In endings, the meeting organizer needs to provide closure for the meeting and create momentum for the next meeting. Without closure, the meeting will feel incomplete. Without connecting it to the next gathering, people would lose momentum for upcoming meetings.

2. Focus, Engagement, and Flow

Meeting participants in a work context want to complete tasks in effective ways as a group. They want the group to perform well. This requires focus and collaboration from everyone. A meeting organizer wants people to feel engaged and have a good experience during a meeting. When people are engaged they get into a state of flow where they enjoy the work to such an extent that they forget the passing of time.

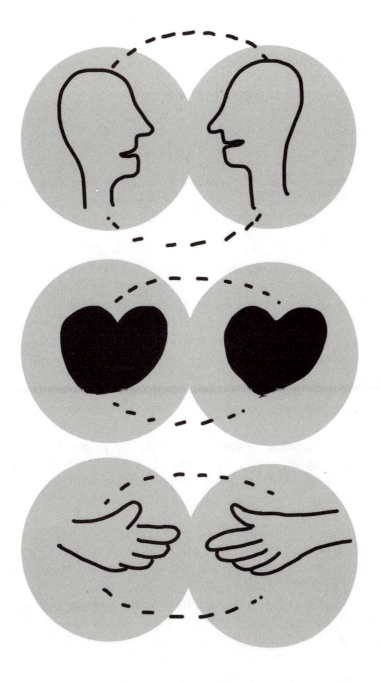

Interactions between people are about establishing connection. Connection can be emotional toward building trust. Connection can also be about creating a shared goal and purpose.

3. Creating Connection and Building Relationships

Two key ingredients of working together well are empathy and trust. Meeting participants need to trust each other to get things done. They further need to empathize with where others stand to better align their goals with them. People can trust and empathize with each other when they know and interact with each other. This requires building connection at a human level which over time turns into strong relationships.

4. Resilience and Rejuvenation

Meeting participants need to manage their energy as they attend many meetings during the workday. They need to recover and bounce back after a long tough meeting. They need to better transition and refresh before entering into the next meeting.

5. Transitions and Shifting Culture

As people join and leave, as projects start and finish, meetings become the transition moments where a team creates memories by celebrating its successes and mourning its losses. Transition moments are also ripe for introducing new values for shifting culture in a team and organization.

These five ritual keys can help the meeting organizer and participants experience a more satisfying meeting. We will showcase rituals for each of these keys in Part 2, Chapters 4 to 9. These rituals are partly from other companies, and partly from our own studio work, covering high-value, high-impact use cases. Before diving into the rituals, we will dig deeper into virtual meetings, and discover the secret science behind virtual meetings in the next chapter.

Nick Fortugno

Game Designer and Educator at Parsons;
CCO of Playmatics LLC

Nick Fortugno is a world-renowned game designer, narrative and story expert, and entrepreneur of digital and real-world games. He is the chief creative officer of Playmatics, which is all about Discovery Through Play, focusing on merging story and interactive experiences in digital and real-world contexts. Nick's game credits include *Diner Dash* and *Ayiti: The Cost of Life.* Nick also teaches game design and interactive narra-tive design at the Columbia School of the Arts Digital Storytelling Lab and at the School of Visual Arts. Nick actually doesn't think of games and ritual as different, seeing games as rituals of play.

Rituals Are Not "Natural"

Nick has intriguing perspectives and strong opinions on rituals. For example, Nick believes that the idea that rituals are intuitive or natural is completely false. In an in-person context, he uses the example of the elbow tap as a greeting, which led him to the handshake as a greeting. When you think about it, there's nothing inherently natural about a handshake! As Nick explains:

"What we don't recognize is that we mistake familiarity with tradition for things that are natural. You can design things in a way that they will become traditions and then they will get that natural feeling. But what makes them work … it's reversing the causality. Things lasted as traditions because they were effective at what they did at one point, and then they became embedded and then that became a reinforcer that eventually might even become … a default that everyone just follows as opposed to being a thoughtful, meaningful practice that relates to the person."

As we are creating new rituals and norms that work in the context of virtual, it helps to keep this in mind.

Play on the Aesthetic Experience

Another one of Nick's concepts that is useful to consider in designing virtual meetings is to think about the aesthetic experience. Nick uses the example of designing "serious games," games designed for a purpose other than pure entertainment (e.g. games designed to promote better health habits). Nick will tell you that "the game doesn't care" about the serious purpose. Instead, people will keep engaging with a serious game that creates a compelling aesthetic experience and facilitates game play. We can apply this concept: Rituals in virtual meetings can help provide better aesthetic experiences and play.

For more on how Nick's ideas can apply to virtual meetings, see the "Are You Game?" section of Chapter 3.

3

The Secret Science of Virtual Meetings

"I have to reframe how I even think about using all of this technology. I find myself asking all kinds of fundamental questions. And as I do that, I eventually realize that the lenses I'm looking through to see the world around me are wrong — and that I have to construct a whole new frame of reference."
– John Seely Brown

The year 2020 may be remembered as the year that everyone realized that videoconferencing technology at the time was kind of ... awkward. Instead of being seen as a technological marvel that kept us connected in a pandemic, media coverage skewed toward portraying videoconferencing as part of the reason why the world was terrible.

Zoom went from feeling like a minor miracle that kept latency under the 150-millisecond "unnatural feeling" threshold to simply feeling unnatural as people started doing everything on Zoom. The phrases "Zoom fatigue" and "Zoomed out" and "Oh no, not another Zoom" entered our lexicon.

There was article after article about why Zoom sucks. Those articles had common themes such as Zoom not accounting for cues, synchrony and mimicry (how humans synchronize and mimic each other), eye contact, who's where in the grid, and constantly seeing yourself. There were many articles and posts on Zoom tips and tricks, which were mostly tactical in nature, covering topics such as muting, turning video on or off, turning off your self view, looking at the camera, using the waiting room, changing display name, and using virtual backgrounds.

However, there weren't as many pieces dedicated to a practical, forward-looking question: *What if we could design our virtual lives to feel more human?*

We can make virtual more human by understanding our underlying needs. We can combine that understanding with insights from a variety of fields on how we experience the world. Those fields include moviemaking, cognitive science, and game design. Through this combination, we can understand virtual rituals that can lead to more satisfying ways of interacting that produce real results.

Technology: Natural vs. Familiar

Before we get into that combination, let's consider a couple of technologies and the effects some argue those technologies have had:

Technology #1: Some argue that this technology has made people more solitary and less likely to spend time with friends. That it has made us more individualistic and fragmented. That it has narrowed us, taking us out of the world of nature and society. That it has biased us toward only one of our senses and eroded our experience of other senses.

Technology #2: Some argue that this technology has grabbed our attention with notifications that pique our curiosity, compelling us to check because we want to find out who and what it is. That it has led to rampant rudeness and led to the decline of civility and courtesy. That it has collapsed the spatial sense that we have of each other.

Technology #1 is the printing press. Technology #2 is the telephone (Lafrance, 2015).

Why bring these up? As we learn how to better navigate an increasingly virtual world and its technologies, it helps to remind ourselves that *it can take time for people and society to get comfortable with a technology and develop norms around its use.*

We can have a tendency to romanticize the comfortably familiar and demonize the uncomfortably unfamiliar. For example, today we might wax nostalgic about the ease of good old-fashioned telephone calls. However, when the telephone first came out, people might have found a greeting of "hello" to be awkward (Lasar, 2010). (Before the phone, people were used to knowing who they were addressing and what time it was for them, and they could greet them more personally, e.g. "Good afternoon, Doctor," instead of a vague "Hello.")

Or as another example, today we might complain that people over-rely

on writing (e.g. texting) and don't spend enough time talking. But at another point in history, when the phone was new, people were complaining about people starting to over-rely on talking (on the phone) and not spending enough time writing (letters) to each other.

There's nothing inherently natural about technology, whether it's videoconferencing, phones, or pens and paper. (Yes, pens and paper are technologies!) To be sure, there are some technologies that are designed in ways that are more intuitive and some that are designed in ways that are less intuitive. We should also recognize that different technologies predispose us in different ways. For example, if you spend 8 hours reading a book, that is likely solitary time that you're not spending with friends.

The point we underline here is that many communications technologies take time for society to get used to. Rituals can help provide support and scaffolding as we get used to less familiar technologies and less familiar ways of interacting.

What makes something feel human?

As we navigate the less familiar, one of the first questions to ask is: *What can make an experience "feel human?"*

For virtual meetings, the first answer that comes to mind might be, "It's just like in-person." But if we reflect a little more deeply, that might not quite be it. We have all been to in-person meetings that weren't exactly the most humanizing experiences. For example, we've all been to some meetings that were monotonous, robotic, stifling, boring, and meaningless – not exactly the epitome of "feel human."

Let's unpack what might make an interaction experience feel more human:

- **We want to be able to express ourselves.** Sometimes we want to express something to the whole group. Sometimes we want to express something to a particular person. (For example, giving someone the "we're on the same wavelength" expression.)

- **We want to feel seen and heard.** At the same time, we don't want to be too self-conscious of how others perceive us.

- **We want to have a sense of what others are really feeling and thinking.** We want to move through something together, and share our reactions and thoughts.

- **We want to be able to shift our attention.** We want to be able to direct and guide attention – and have our attention directed and guided – in helpful ways.

- **We want to avoid being rude or insensitive.** We want our intentions to be understood.

Humans have been interacting in-person for 200,000 years, and various cultures around the world have developed conventions that help people meet the needs above in in-person interactions. On the other hand, the world's first popular web browser was released in 1993, so we can be gentle on ourselves for not yet having virtual fully figured out.

There are different fields that can help us find better ways of interacting virtually. Let's start with one of the oldest fields that involves portraying things on a screen – moviemaking.

Shift How We See

Screen fatigue is a very real thing, people in 2020 were exposed to a heavy dose of it as everyone was forced to rely more heavily on interactions on screens. But did you ever notice that some screens fatigue and other screens intrigue? For example, perhaps you weren't all that likely to be feeling screen fatigue when watching a 90-minute movie – or 5 straight hours of Netflix binging – even if you were watching on a laptop.

Part of this has to do with the amount of focus expected for meetings versus movies. With meetings, we're expected to pay attention. With movies, we can veg out if we want to. Ironically though, we may end up engaging more in movies than in meetings! So there are other factors at play.

One factor is something that movies have in common with narrative books and radio shows, and we'll talk about that shortly. But first, let's talk about a factor that is specific to movies.

Try this exercise – watch any movie for 3 minutes, and count the number of times it cuts from one camera angle to another. You might be surprised at just how many cuts there are. James Cutting (his real name!), a psychologist at Cornell University who studies film, has shown how the average shot length in English language films is around 2.5 seconds today (Miller, 2014).

Now you might be thinking, "Oh, the insight for virtual meetings is going to be that we constantly need to rapidly cut from view to view to keep giving people dopamine hits so they don't get bored!" That's a reasonable guess, but that's ... not it at all. The insight is more profound. The reason why film cuts work tells us something about how we see the world, and this will give us clues for better virtual meetings.

The way we see the world is not passive. Our vision is active, with our eyes moving around to scan our environment and take in what's around us. Our vision is predictive, and we look around to check our predictions. ("I bet that comment Steve made is going to annoy the big boss. [Eyes shift to the boss.] Yep, yep, yep ... she is livid.") Our eyes don't naturally fixate on a single thing.

Film editing takes advantage of how we perceive things every day — editing in many ways emulates how our attention constantly shifts while maintaining continuity across those shifts. We are constantly shifting our attention through things like rapid eye movements called saccades.

Jeff Zacks, author of *Flicker: Your Brain on Movies*, puts it this way: "A great filmmaker is a great intuitive psychologist. They are giving you the sequence of fixations that you, or at least the views that you would have, if you could move your head and your body around" (Zacks, 2014).

The great film editor, Walter Murch, gives this example: "If you're observing a dialogue between two people, you will not focus your attention solely on the person who is speaking. Instead, while that person is still talking, you will turn to look at the listener to find out what he thinks of what is being said. The question is, 'When exactly do you turn?'" As Murch notes, "the cut – the sudden switch from one image to another – mimics the acrobatic nature of thought itself." Murch also describes how cinema's power comes from the combination of the cut and the close-up shot, where we can see subtleties of expression quickly (Murch, 2001).

Think about your most recent in-person meeting. Most likely, you were not staring at one person's face for 30 minutes straight. This would be socially awkward in-person, perhaps borderline creepy. Now think about what many webinars look like: a disembodied voice talking over a bunch of slides. It also does not allow you to shift your attention.

If we don't shift our attention, we can feel trapped and monotonous. We can burn out by focusing on something too much (e.g. staring at a person's face continuously, staring at a single slide for a long time).

Building on this insight, we can start to frame this into a challenge: "How might we structure our real-time virtual interactions to enable us and nudge us to shift our attention in desirable ways?"

Let's illustrate with an example.

Imagine you are meeting with several people on a Zoom call. There's a section of the meeting where one person is giving an update where they are talking for about 5 minutes with no slides.

If you watch this continuously on Speaker View in Zoom, there's a good chance you are going to space out at some point. If you watch this continuously in Gallery View, there's also a good chance you are going to space out.

But if you occasionally flip back and forth between Speaker View and Gallery View – say two-thirds Speaker View to watch the speaker, and one-third Gallery View to see different people's reactions – those shifts might help you stay engaged throughout. For more details on this example, check out the Conversation Cuts ritual in Chapter 7.

What's the Story?

A second thing we can learn from movies that helps build intrigue and engagement is something that movies have in common with narrative books and radio shows and podcasts. That something is story structure.

Most stories – whether they are in a movie, book, or radio show – have a shape. You might be familiar with story arcs, like this one.

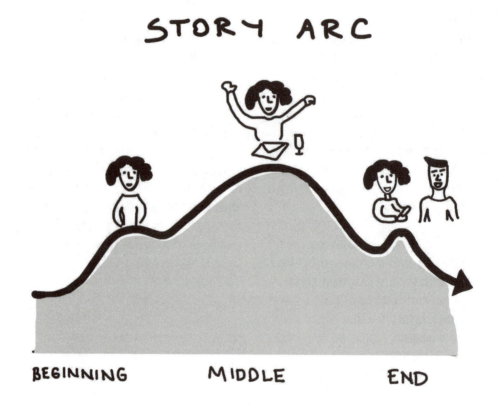

STORY ARC

BEGINNING   MIDDLE   END

In a classic arc, there are characters and a story problem that get introduced, then there's rising action that leads to a climax and resolution.

There are two magical properties of story structure that can help lead us to more engaging virtual meetings:

1. Curiosity
2. Chunking

Many of the rituals in this book will draw on these properties, which are interlinked with each other.

Curiosity

Curiosity can hook us in and keep us in.

Bingeing on Netflix provides a visceral example. You watch the first few minutes of an episode, and you're hooked. Why? You're dropped into a story problem, your curiosity is activated, and you want to know what happens. So you keep watching. Then at the end of the episode, you get some resolution, some satisfaction about the opening story problem. Ahhhh … But then there's a hint about the next problem, and before you know it, you're clicking Next Episode. (And then 6 hours later, you realize that it's 2 in the morning.)

Educator and economist George Loewenstein describes curiosity as "a cognitively induced deprivation that arises from the perception of a gap in knowledge and understanding." Lowenstein compares curiosity to hunger, where we have an urge that we must satisfy "(Loewenstein, 1994).

What if we intentionally tapped into curiosity in our virtual meetings? What if we could spark curiosity about the content and the people in a meeting? Rituals can help with this.

Chunking

We're going to drop a little cognitive science jargon here. Don't worry – we'll bring it back to story structure and practical implications.

Over the past two decades, there has been a growing body of research on how people perceive, remember, think about, and respond to events. In academia, the topical area is called *event cognition*. Our brains make sense of things by creating event models, which are structured representations of events in our heads.

Humans don't remember all the details of everything. Instead, we pick up the gist and remember things as event models, which are simplifications that are good enough for us to be able make inferences to fill gaps in our understanding and to make predictions about what might happen so that we can function in our daily lives.

One function of perception is to divide continuous experience into discrete parts, providing a structure for selective attention, memory, and control. For example, when watching someone boil water, an observer might divide that person's activity into getting a pot from a rack, filling the pot with water, setting the pot on the burner, turning on the burner, and bringing the water to a boil.

The story structure of narrative film, books, and radio shows can help them become more memorable, because they appeal to our model-building tendencies, helping us understand and simulate an event. For example, commercial films help us chunk the visual and auditory signals we get, help guide our attention, and provide cues to trigger chunking (Zacks, 2014). These cues take on a variety of forms, from a wide-angle shot to establish a new scene to a change in background music. Similarly, in books, things are chunked into chapters, which sometimes have additional cues like a first letter's drop cap.

In story structure, surprises or twists and turns are also critical. They lead to what a cognitive scientist would call "useful prediction errors that trigger a new event boundary." This flags us down and gets our attention: "Hey! You thought those were chicken bones, but they're actually parts of a rare dinosaur fossil. This is a different situation than you thought it was." These surprises signal to our brain that we need to update our understanding. There's an important balance with surprises. If everything was a surprise, we would be totally overwhelmed. If nothing was a surprise, we would space out and check out.

We can give special care to the final bit of chunking for a meeting, i.e. the end of a meeting. Satisfying endings are critical to help us make sense of what has transpired. For example, we can draw upon the thinking of radio producer Rob Rosenthal, who believes that there are no rules with endings, but there are tendencies that happen to work. Two that stick out to him are: 1) a moment of reflection where a character provides larger meaning – this is what this experience means to me, how it changed me; 2) a reference to the future, an implication, or what's next (e.g. "in the future … but for now ….").

Chunking helps us make sense of events and remember them. Movies, books, and radio shows use conventions to trigger chunking. And if we're clever, we can trigger chunking in virtual meetings. Rituals can help us with this.

Are You Game?

As we can find inspiration for virtual meetings in movies, we can also find inspiration in the field of game design, including board games, role-playing games, and video games. Well-designed games harmonize structure (object of the game and rules) with spontaneity (how people play). This is not unlike what a good meeting does.

We're going to highlight three concepts of game design that we can apply to virtual meetings, and some of our rituals will be rooted in these concepts.

Enter the Magic Circle

When you start playing a game, whether it's Monopoly or Fortnite, you are entering an alternate world of sorts. This is our first game design concept we can draw upon – the "magic circle." The magic circle is the idea that there's a boundary between the game and the world outside of the game.

Scott Nicholson, owner of a board game café, describes it this way, "You have a social contract when you sit down to play a game." David Sax references ideas of Evan Torner, the editor of *Analog Game Studies*, that a game acts as an alibi for its players to engage in certain behaviors, and game designer Bernie De Koven says that a game "requires a collective investment of your imagination in an alternate reality to believe that you actually own Park Avenue" (Sax, 2016).

What if we treated meetings as if they had a magic circle and we entered a different world together? What if we elevated meetings as moments where we could harness our collective talent?

When we spoke with game designer Nick Fortugno and he considered how we might apply the magic circle to virtual meetings, he reflected, "Magic circles need to be clear. They have to be very clear, right? One of the problems with a lot of these virtual meeting spaces is that they start sloppy and they end sloppy." If we can create clearer beginnings and endings, we can elevate our meeting space. Rituals can help with this.

Rules and Game Play

We might also draw inspiration for virtual meetings from how games are structured, with clarity around the object of the game and the rules of the game, but freedom to play within those constraints. Structuring with this concept in mind can help bring out everyone's best thinking.

As Nick Fortugno shared, "I think that my goal as a game designer is not to tell you what to do. My goal in this game is to tell you what you can't do and what you're trying to do. And then what you do, you figure out, right? And that's where the game gets interesting … We want people to be creative because that creativity is the fun of the game."

Nick and other game designers will tell you that if you don't let people make any decisions or if you don't give them challenges to tackle, they probably won't feel compelled by the game. And if the object or rules of the game are unclear, people are less likely to be compelled by the game. We can draw inspiration from game structure for virtual meetings, and rituals can help with this.

Game structure can also help us balance risk and safety within a meeting experience. Experience designer Ida Benedetto thinks of it this way: "My thesis is that for an experience to be transformative, it needs some element of real risk. And that the whole point of the experience is it makes it possible to approach that risk in a safer way that you couldn't do without the supportive structure of the experience." We can use this type of mindset for our virtual meetings.

Can you affordance it?

A third concept we can draw from game design (as well as other design fields) is the idea of affordances. The definition of affordances that is most relevant for our purposes is from Don Norman, author of *The Design of Everyday Things*. Affordances are action possibilities that are available to a person (Norman, 2013).

Sometimes those action possibilities are more apparent, sometimes they are less apparent. For example, if you had a piece of paper, it's commonly known that you can write on it. It's less obvious, but not that much a stretch to see that it's possible to make a paper airplane and throw it at your friend to get their attention. It is quite a stretch to see that it's possible to use a piece of paper to open a beer bottle, but it is possible!

We can find new action possibilities with what we have available to us.

Parentheses and semicolons probably were not designed for you to be sly, but someone figured this out. ;)

We can draw inspiration from how people find creative uses of affordances. For example, *Fortnite* is a shooter game where you can move through worlds and the point of the game is to survive. It happens to have dances so that players can be more expressive. Over time, rapper Travis Scott and his team figured out how to do a massive concert tour in *Fortnite* (Webster, 2020).

You don't have to have an audience of 27.7 million unique visitors like Travis Scott to find creative uses of affordances that you do have available to you in a virtual meeting. The key is to **avoid a deficiency mindset**. Don't get stuck on what you don't have available in virtual that you do have available in person. Instead, **flip it to a generative mindset**. As you explore what you *can* do, think of it as a game you are playing. Get curious about what you do have available in virtual that you might not have available in person.

Here are two examples:

Example 1: In a virtual meeting, you always have a close-up shot available of each person who has video on in the meeting. For example, in Zoom, you can use Pin Video in Speaker View to pick up even more subtlety of facial expression of people's reactions.

Example 2: Consider different ways you can use virtual backgrounds in Zoom in practical ways. For example, you can create a custom background in Google Slides or PowerPoint and export the slide you make as an image file that can be used as a virtual background. To illustrate one practical application, your meeting attendees could use a simple color code of virtual backgrounds to indicate how they are feeling about the topic at hand (e.g. green = I'm good, let's move forward; yellow = I'm unsure about things; red = I have a significant concerns that I'd like to address). For another example, see the Background Together ritual in Chapter 7.

A Whole New World

This joke is so bad that we're going to warn you that it's a joke and that it's bad:

Question: What do you get when you combine movies with the concept of building alternate worlds from game design?

Answer: A whole new world. (Don't you dare close your eyes.)

Ahem. Um, yes. Instead of ending on that stinker, let's recap what we've explored in Chapter 3.

We started with a practical, forward-looking question: What if we could design our virtual lives to feel more human?

We reminded ourselves that it can take time for people and society to get comfortable with a technology and develop norms around its use.

We considered what can make an experience "feel human." This includes being able to express yourself, feel seen and heard, sense what others are thinking and feeling, move through things together, be able to shift our attention, and have our intentions understood.

Then we dove into what we can learn from moviemaking, cognitive science, and game design to create better virtual meetings.

We can learn from cuts in movies, as they reveal how we see the world. Our vision is active and predictive. We scan and shift our attention to answer our questions.

We can learn from the story structure that movies, narrative books, and radio shows and podcasts use. We can learn from how story structure continually draws us in with curiosity. We can learn from how story structure provides chunking that helps us build models in our heads that we're more likely to remember.

We can learn from different concepts of game design. We can learn from the concept of a magic circle of a game, where we enter a different world together. We can learn from rules and game play, how they balance structure with freedom to inspire creative play. And we can learn from the concept of affordances, to prompt us to think about the action possibilities that we are making available to our meeting participants.

Many of the rituals in Parts 2 and 3 of this book build on these insights. And you can use these insights in your own ways as you create better virtual meetings.

Given how the world has unfolded, we can't go back to where we used to be. There are new horizons to pursue. If we have a forward-looking and generative mindset, ideas from moviemaking, cognitive science, and game design can open us up to a new fantastic point of view for virtual meetings. What if a virtual meeting could be a wondrous place for you and me?

Jeff Zacks

Professor of Psychological and Brain
Sciences Professor of Radiology

How Brain Science Can Inform Virtual Rituals

Jeff Zacks is a professor of psychological and brain sciences at Washington University who studies perception and cognition using behavioral experiments, functional MRI, computational modeling, and testing of neurological patients. His Dynamic Cognition Laboratory studies how the representations in the brain and the world work together in cognition. Jeff is the author of several books, including *Flicker: Your Brain on Movies*.

Making Models

Jeff's work on how we perceive the world has important implications for the usefulness of rituals and design of rituals, particularly in a virtual context. For example, Jeff talks about how our brains make sense of the world by constructing event models:

To understand a story, we construct models of the story's events. An event model is a representation in your head that corresponds systematically to the situation in the story. It is not a perfect copy – it simplifies a lot and distorts some things, but it is accurate enough that you can use it to run simulations that can tell you about parts of the situation you may have missed and to infer what might happen soon.

Jeff's insights suggest that part of the power of rituals comes from their potential to help shape how our brain forms event models, as we process what is going on in a meeting. For example, a ritual can provide more obvious cues on event boundaries – e.g. the beginning or end of something – and those mental guideposts can help people feel more oriented in a meeting.

Jeff's work on the effects of movies on our brains has important applicability to virtual rituals and virtual collaboration in general. For example, Jeff describes how movies use various devices to direct our attention and help us chunk streams of information into pieces our brains can more easily absorb. (For more on chunking, see "What's the Story?" section of Chapter 3.)

What you want to see in the world

Jeff's detailed analysis of why film cuts work – how they mirror how our active vision takes in the world – can help us create better virtual collaboration experiences. We don't naturally stare at a single view for an extended amount of time. Instead, we're often scanning around to find answers for our questions. For example: "I wonder if that will annoy the boss? Yep, he's clearly frustrated." Or: "I forget – what was net revenue in Q4? Ah, here it is in the chart." If

we use this concept, we can consider all the different things that people in a meeting might want to be able to see, and then structure the meeting experience accordingly. (For more on this topic, see "Shift How We See" in Chapter 3.)

Be scene

One last example we can apply is from research about scene structure that Jeff cites from James Cutting: "If you average over many, many films [over different] variables, you see some consistent temporal structure that is consistent with a three act or a four act kind of structure" (Miller, 2014). We can use this type of consistent structure to help orient people in meetings. (The Opening Scene ritual in Chapter 4 is an example of this.)

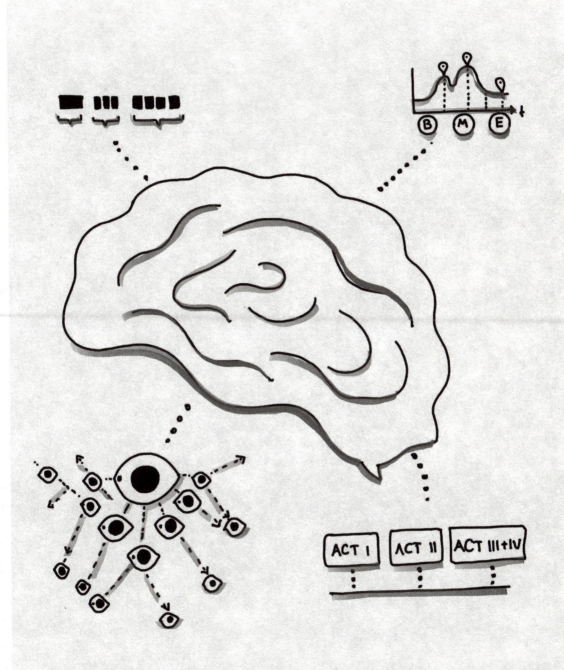

PART TWO

Rituals for Virtual Meetings

4

Rituals for Beginning and Ending a Meeting with Engagement

"How do I make it less awkward?"

Beginning and Ending Rituals

These rituals help bring a narrative arc to a virtual meeting, with transitions that help participants make sense of what's happening, mark the start and end of the experience, and adapt to the different roles they may take on during the session.

"In the first few moments of a gathering, we are reading cues and asking ourselves: What do I think of this gathering? Am I in good hands? Is the host nervous? Should I be? What's going to happen here? Is this worth my time? Do I belong? Do I want to belong? The opening is, therefore, an important opportunity to establish the legitimacy of your gathering."
– Priya Parker

Have you ever found the start and end of virtual meetings to be a little weird? Perhaps awkward? Or just kind of odd?

At the start, people gradually show up. Maybe people say hello. Or maybe they don't, particularly if it's a larger meeting. Eventually, someone says, "Okay, let's begin ..." Some people try to politely look like they are paying attention, but you can see the uncertain awkwardness in their faces. Other people's minds are clearly elsewhere, perhaps the meeting they just finished or something they have to prep for later in the day. It might take a while for people to get their minds completely into the meeting, if they do so at all.

At the end, perhaps someone says, "Ah, we're at time, we should end," and people hurry off. Or perhaps the meeting goes past time and you start wondering if the meeting will end. Maybe there is a recap of next steps that feels practical, but not exactly inspiring. Then people either disappear or wave goodbye.

What if beginnings and endings could feel less awkward and more awesome? What if they felt less inelegant and more invigorating?

The rituals in Chapter 4 can help. Choose rituals that work for your specific contexts and situations. Adopt and adapt rituals as you see fit.

Hi By Name makes people feel welcome from the moment they join. **Guided Breathing** helps a group enter into the same mental space together. **Detailed Inquiry** give group members a sense each other's current frame of mind. **Last Line** can get people smiling and laughing from the start. **Opening Scene** can drop a group into the story of that meeting. **On Purpose** helps people understand each other's goals. **Parting A-ha** surfaces what people learned in a meeting. **PDA (Public Display of Appreciation)** helps us close with gratitude.

8 Rituals for Beginning and Ending a Meeting with Engagement

01 Hi By Name
Greet Each Other Personally

02 Guided Breathing
Center Together and Get in Sync

03 Detailed Inquiry
Connect Before Jumping into Business

04 Last Line
Begin with a Funny End

05 Opening Scene
Drop People into a Story and Create Suspense

06 On Purpose
Understand Each Person's Goals

07 Parting A-ha
Share Sparks of Insights

08 PDA (Public Display of Appreciation)
Express Gratitude in Front of the Group

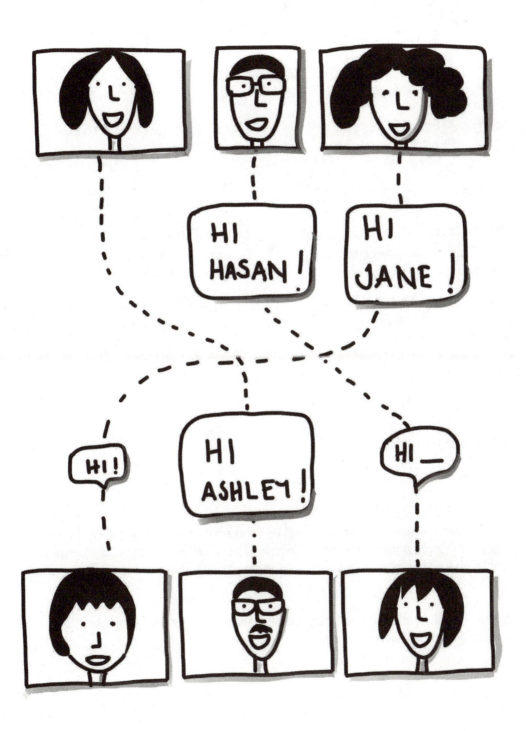

01 Hi By Name

Moment
At the beginning of a meeting.

This ritual is best with **5 to 20 people.**

Intention
Make participants feel welcome and connect with each other.

Time & Effort
Takes 2–3 minutes to do (30 seconds to give instructions, then 5 seconds per person to say hi).

What is the ritual?

"First moments matter." – Jane Dutton

Who doesn't enjoy a warm personal welcome when entering a room full of people? People appreciate being seen and noticed. This is especially important in virtual team meetings where people cannot easily see each other and read the room.

In this ritual, everyone gets greeted personally. The underlying intention is to create a foundation for connection.

Backstory

Jane Dutton emphasizes the importance of people feeling welcome, for people to feel that someone else is glad that they are present. When Jane is leading virtual meetings, she makes it a point to greet everyone by name as they join the meeting. "Hi Frank! Hi Natasha! Hi Pat!"

Glenn created Hi By Name as a variation of what Jane does. Instead of having the meeting facilitator greet everyone, each person is greeted by someone and then greets someone else, creating a verbal "hi" circle with the entire group.

This variation helps us feel like we're all responsible for making each other feel welcome, and the little bit of participation of saying "hi" helps get people's brains into the meeting. That "hi" cues us. We're now actively together.

This variation works better with groups of 5 to 20 people. With groups that are much larger, it gets to be on the long side and it gets trickier to remember who has not yet been greeted. (If you'd like, after someone has been greeted and has said hi to someone else, you can have them hold up their hand in a frozen hand wave position, so it's easier to tell who has already gone.)

Why are knowing and recognizing people's names so important? Names are part of people's core identity. When people talk to each other with their names, the familiarity kicks in, and people can build rapport and trust on that familiarity.

How it works

The meeting facilitator gives the following instructions once everyone who we think is going to join is on the call.

1. "Let's start. I'm going to say hi to one person by name."

2. "Then that person will say hi to another person by name, and so on."

3. "Don't say hi to anyone who someone else has already said hi to. The idea is that everyone gets greeted by name once.

4. "Be enthusiastic and keep it snappy; let's try to get a rhythm going."

5. "When we reach the last person, that person says hi to me."

After the last person says hi to the meeting facilitator, the facilitator thanks the group and immediately goes into the next item on the meeting agenda.

Hi By Name can also become Bye By Name, where everyone gets a personal farewell.

02 Guided Breathing

Moment
At the beginning of a meeting.

This ritual can be done with **small and large groups.**

Intention
Prime people to be present.

Time & Effort
Takes 3–5 minutes to run the ritual.

What is the ritual?

Have you ever been to meetings where people arrive but their minds are elsewhere, perhaps in whatever they were doing right before the meeting?

Rather than diving into agenda items right away, this ritual starts the meeting with a guided breathing activity to prime people to be present, listen, and notice others in the meeting.

After everyone has joined the call, the meeting organizer sets a timer and invites people to a breathing activity with a countdown. Once started, the organizer can guide participants on breathing in and out. As the timer goes off, the organizer can close the activity with a well-wish, such as "have a bright day ahead!"

Once you're comfortable with the basic version, you can create more variety by playing with the length of the activity, or adding audio and visual backgrounds during the breathing.

Backstory

We learned about this ritual from Marica Rizzo, community manager at Acumen, a global anti-poverty organization. Acumen found when people join virtual meetings, they often don't have a physical change of place (e.g. entering a conference room), so they don't have cues that tell people, "You are leaving one mental space and entering a different space."

So they use this ritual to provide a transition experience. Marica calls it "re-presencing" each time you jump from one virtual meeting to another.

How it works

1. Ask everyone to get comfortable where they are sitting, ideally with their feet planted on the floor.

2. Ask everyone to close their eyes.

3. Explain what they're about to do and why: "We're starting with a guided breathing warm-up to transition from what we were doing before this meeting, to being fully present in this meeting."

4. Explain how they will breathe together: "We'll first breathe in through our nose and fill our lungs with air. We'll do that for four counts. Then we will breathe out through our mouth and push all of the air out of our lungs. We'll do that for four counts as well."

5. Start breathing: "Let's start! Breathe in through your nose. One, two, three four. Hold for four seconds, Now breathe out through your mouth. One, two, three, four. And finally hold for four seconds."

6. Repeat this breathe in, breathe out cycle. Do this for a total of four times, which will take about 40–60 seconds total. At Acumen, they call it 4X4.

7. Close the activity: "Thank you everyone. Now that we're all present together, let's begin with our meeting agenda."

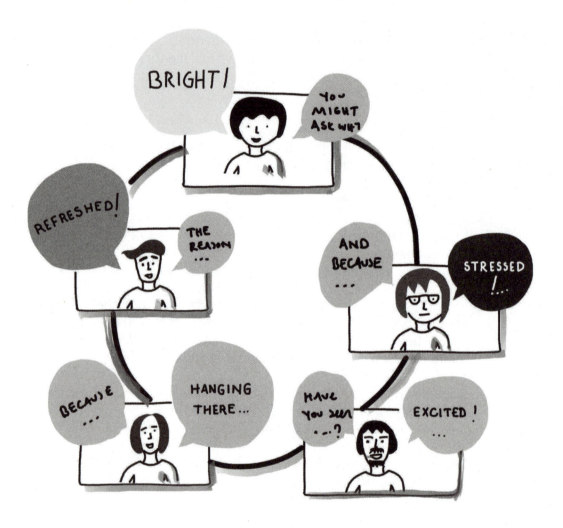

03 Detailed Inquiry

Moment

At the beginning of a meeting.

This is a **small group ritual.**

Intention

Foster connection, to encourage vulnerability and a sense of unity and support in a fast-changing world.

Time & Effort

Allow 2 minutes for instructions, 1 minute per person to share, and 1 minute to wrap up.

What is the ritual?

Have you ever felt alone in a room full of your peers? Do you feel like you're the only one experiencing hardship or even euphoria in an evolving world? Do you feel like the question "How are you?" is an empty formality and that no one actually wants to know how you feel?

With Detailed Inquiry, you'll feel a sense of community and the backstories will prompt you to empathize and sympathize with your colleagues. At the beginning of the meeting, each person thinks about one word to summarize their general mood then goes into detail about what has informed their feelings. The time limit for each person is dependent on the number of participants in the meeting.

The organizer asks how everyone is doing, explains that this is not a judgmental space and that all feelings are valid and each person gets to share in the order designated by the organizer.

A word to the wise: Although this exercise encourages vulnerability, it is important to consider how much honesty or openness might be too much, particularly in professional settings. The backstory for your feelings is not an excuse to make the rest of the meeting attendees feel awkward and uncomfortable. A quick appraisal of the crowd and the purpose of the meeting goes a long way!

Backstory

We learned about this ritual from Alundrah Sibanda, the co-founder of Shielded Africa, a continental organization whose mandate is to fight Gender-Based Violence in Africa. In her work, Alundrah meticulously crafts safe and empowering spaces for survivors of gender-based violence. The Detailed Inquiry ritual provides a glimpse into her approach.

How it works

1. This takes place at the beginning of the meeting and a minute is more than enough time for each person to share their detailed answer. Everyone on the call should be muted when a participant is sharing to avoid any verbal real-time reactions.

2. Instructions from the moderator may resemble this: "As we begin this meeting, I'd like everyone to share how they are really feeling. In under 1 minute, use one word to describe how you are feeling and give us a backstory that you're comfortable with sharing in this meeting. This is a non-judgmental space and all feelings are valid. Please mute your mics while each participant shares their feelings and story."

3. The moderator must set an example by sharing his/her/their own feeling/emotion word and story/supporting experience.

4. Call on each person to share. Perhaps use alphabetical order so that no one feels singled out and there are no awkward silences.

5. After everyone shares their feelings, give the group an additional minute to think about and reflect on all the feelings represented in the room, how they empathize or sympathize with others in the group, and how fascinating it is that people living through the same unpredictable period can experience and react to it in such varied and diverse ways.

6. Start the formal proceedings after the minute of reflection.

04 Last Line

Moment
Near the start of a meeting where you need everyone to contribute ideas.

This is a **small group ritual.**

Intention
Help people feel comfortable and confident in sharing ideas.

Time & Effort
Can be done in as little as 3 minutes when using chat. Takes a bit longer with quick shares out loud.

What is the ritual?

Sometimes you'll have a meeting with a group of people where not everyone is comfortable sharing their thoughts or ideas. Last Line is a lighthearted activity that gets people comfortable with creating and sharing.

People think of one awkward experience that they've had in the last month or so. They quickly think about how they would tell the story of that experience. Then they're told that they don't have to tell the whole story, but instead just have to share the very last line of the story, using this prompt: "But it turns out that _____ "

These last lines are shared with the group and hilarity ensues.

Backstory

Last Line was created by Glenn in Design Across Borders, a Stanford d.school class. There was one class session where students were preparing to share stories from the interviews they conducted, about moments when something clicked for them. The subject material could be quite uncomfortable and heavy. Students were exploring political polarization by interviewing people they strongly disagreed with.

To warm students up for this, Glenn created an activity where they shared something from another uncomfortable experience they had that was probably more lighthearted.

Many of the last lines that students shared were quite funny and also sparked a lot of curiosity ("Oh, I want to hear that story!"). Glenn realized that Last Line could be used not only to prepare people for sharing stories, but could more generally be used to get people comfortable sharing their ideas.

Glenn thinks there are three reasons why Last Line works. First, if I can get comfortable sharing something from an awkward experience, I'll probably feel comfortable sharing my other thoughts. Second, it helps foster mutual curiosity – I realize people might be interested in what I have to say and that I might be interested in what other people have to say. Third, it can prime people to share ideas with an eye toward practical implications – why does it matter?

How it works

1. The meeting facilitator quickly sets the context: "To warm us up, we're going to do a quick activity called Last Line."
2. Then the facilitator asks everyone to think of one thing that happened to them: "What is one awkward thing that happened to you in the last month or so?"
3. The facilitator asks people to quickly think about how they'd tell the story of what happened: "I'm going to give you 30 seconds to think about how you'd tell the story of what happened."
4. Then the facilitator has people formulate what they will share: "Okay, now think, what would be the last line of that story, if that line used this prompt: 'But it turns out that _____'"
5. Depending on the size of the group, sharing can be done either out loud or typed into a chat.

05 Opening Scene

Moment
Opening of a meeting where a group is just starting a new project.

This ritual can work in **small and large groups.**

Intention
Get people's attention at the start of a meeting where you are tackling a specific challenge together.

Time & Effort
Before the meeting, 10 minutes to think about your story. During the meeting, takes 2–5 minutes to tell your story.

What is the ritual?

Start your meeting like a movie or Netflix episode that hooks people in from the start. Think of your meeting as a story with a plot, characters, and a setting. Develop a "story problem" that is the central challenge for this meeting. Create curiosity and suspense.

What is something that we will tackle in this meeting, something that people care about, that has some uncertainty? How could this be posed as a suspenseful, but doable challenge for the group?

Open your meeting with that opening scene to get people engaged.

Backstory

This was developed by Glenn for one of his classes.

How it works

1. Before your meeting, imagine your meeting as a mini-movie or a Net-flix episode. Consider:

    Characters: How can you make the people in your meeting the he-roes, the main characters of the story? And what other characters are critical to the story? (e.g. key stakeholders)

    Story Problem: What is the specific challenge you're tackling? Why does it matter? What makes it difficult?

    Setting: What is the organizational or market backdrop for the chal-lenge you're tackling? Paint a picture of the context and constraints.

    Plot: What is the journey that the characters are going to take to tackle the story problem? What's the suspense, what are the uncer-tainties about how the plot is going to unfold?

2. Now think about what the first few minutes of this movie or episode looks like. What is the opening scene that drops people into the story and creates curiosity?

3. At the beginning of the meeting, in 2–5 minutes, tell the story of this opening scene, to set up a narrative of what's going to unfold in this meeting.

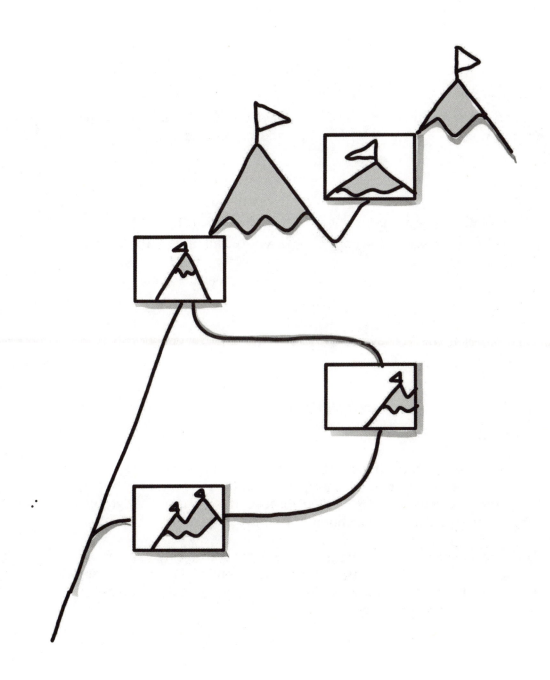

06 On Purpose

Moment
At start of the meeting and end of the meeting.

This ritual can be done with **small and large groups**.

Intention
Understand why each of the participants is there.

Time & Effort
Takes 2–3 minutes at the beginning of a meeting, and 1–2 minutes at the end. Keep it snappy.

What is the ritual?

Sometimes we go through the motions with meetings, and we join with only an abstract sense of "we should meet" or simply because someone put an appointment on our calendar. The On Purpose ritual focuses your group on why you are spending these minutes of your lives together.

At the beginning of the meeting, people consider and quickly share what they are hoping to get out of the meeting. At the end of the meeting, people share what they did and did not get out of the meeting, and any next step they will take to address their unmet needs.

Backstory

On Purpose was inspired by different facilitators' approaches to checking and setting expectations at the beginning of a meeting. Glenn adds a "10 words or less" constraint to keep it snappy and easier to remember.

How it works

1. At the start of the meeting, ask: "Why are you here at this meeting? Given the topic, what's the most important thing you're hoping to get out of our time together? Write it down in 10 words or less."

2. Give people 30 seconds to think about it.

3. Then have people very quickly share.
   - If it's a smaller group, sharing can be done verbally. Call on people to keep it moving. Politely intervene if someone is going way beyond 10 words.
   - If it's a large group, sharing can be done in the videoconference chat.

4. Based on what people have shared, to calibrate expectations, quickly comment on what will and will not be addressed in this meeting. For example, "We're not going to have a detailed plan in the next 30 minutes, but we will get crystal clear on the priorities and constraints that will drive that plan."

5. Then at the end of meeting, ask everyone to quickly share what they did and did not get out of the meeting, and any next step they will take to address their unmet needs.

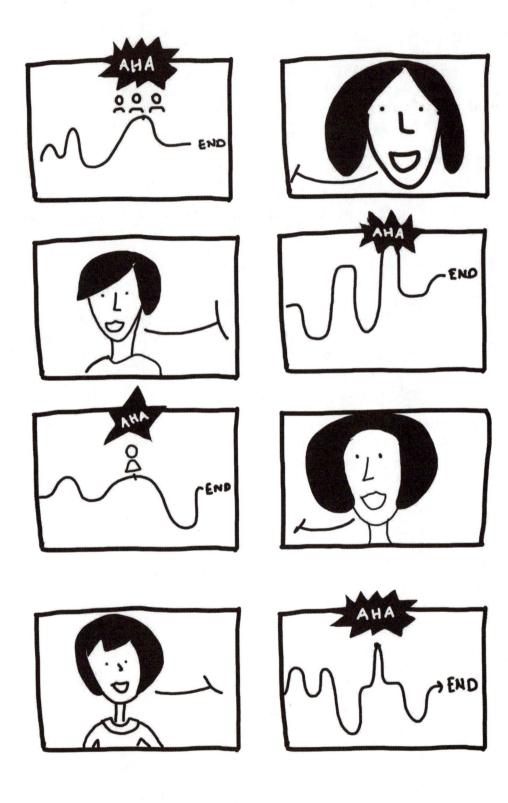

07 Parting A-ha

Moment

At the end of any meeting or event.

This can be a **small and large group ritual.**

Intention

Reflect on the meeting, and understand one thing each person got out of it.

Time & Effort

This is an easy ritual to set up. Depending on the time, you can spend 1 minute for people to put it on chat, or 5 minutes to share out.

What is the ritual?

Did you ever come away from a meeting and you weren't sure what each person got out of it? With the Parting A-ha ritual, you'll know at least one takeaway for each person!

At the end of a meeting, each person thinks about one a-ha they had from the meeting, one thing they're walking away with, or a new perspective they now have. Each person shares their a-ha with the group as a one or two sentence reflection.

The meeting organizer opens up the floor for a round of reflection. People take turns and say it verbally or write them in a chat window.

Backstory

Parting A-ha comes from Acumen, a global anti-poverty organization. Acumen has used this since its founding; being reflective is one of Acumen's core values. When they perform this ritual in every meeting, they reinforce their identity as staff, as community members, as teammates. (They capture a-ha's in their meeting minutes too!) Being reflective for them means balancing the being out in the world, acting, and taking action to create change, and reflecting on those actions as individual change agents and leaders.

How it works

1. This activity takes place at the end of a meeting and you want to make sure you save enough time to make it worthwhile. You will need about 15 seconds for each person in your group to share, and an additional minute to guide the activity, For example, if you have 8 people in the meeting you will need to save 3 minutes at the end of the meeting (8 people x 15 seconds + 1 minute for guiding the group).

2. Give instructions to the group: "As we close this meeting, I'd like to ask everyone to think of one a-ha that you have from this meeting. What's one thing you are walking away with or a new perspective you now have? Be ready to share with the group briefly, in one or two sentences."

3. Call on each person to share their a-ha. (One variant, instead of the meeting facilitator calling on each person, after a person shares their a-ha, that person calls on another person who has not yet shared an a-ha.)

4. When everyone has shared an a-ha, close the meeting by thanking the group as a whole and making a hand gesture of thanks (e.g. open hands, palms facing each other, pressed together – a Thai wai gesture).

08 PDA (Public Display of Appreciation)

Moment
At a major milestone or the end of a project or event.

This ritual can be done in **small and large groups.**

Intention
Express gratitude for each other.

Time & Effort
Takes 4–7 minutes, depending on size of group and how sharing is done.

What is the ritual?

"Thank you" never goes out of style. In work life, many people simply do not get thanked enough. This simple ritual is about praise in public.

Each person in the group thanks at least one other person in the group in a **specific** and **personal** way. The idea is to help the group see and honor each person's contributions.

With groups of 15 people or less, this can be done in a real-time video conference. With larger groups, people can record their messages on video.

Backstory

This ritual started in the Borderless Youth Forum, a global virtual conference for young people to engage in justice issues. In October 2019, the Forum had 138 participants from 55 countries across the Eastern Hemisphere, with participants doing much of their work in small multinational teams of 4 to 5 people each.

The Borderless organizers prioritize human connection and relationship building throughout the experience, and one of the most memorable moments was the Public Display of Appreciation near the close of the Forum, where teammates thanked each other in a place where everyone could see. At a designated time, every Forum participant recorded a video message that was less than 60 seconds long on WhatsApp and posted to the "All Forum" WhatsApp Group.

Teammates were touched across thousands of miles by each other's video messages. Participants also browsed messages across teams to get inspired by what had transpired in the broader Forum community.

How it works

1. This ritual is done near the end of a meeting that marks a major milestone, or the end of a project or event.

2. Tell people who they should make sure to thank (e.g. the people they worked with the most). You want to structure so that everyone in the group receives thanks from at least one person.

3. Give people 1 minute to think about what are going to say: "We want you to thank others in specific and personal ways. Think about what you want to thank this person for. Show that you noticed what exactly they did to help others."

4. For smaller groups, you might have people take turns expressing their thanks in real-time on a video call. For larger groups, we recommend that thank-you messages are recorded in video and shared as video messages (e.g. in a WhatsApp group) or in a shared gallery (e.g. a Shared album in Google Photos). It's also possible to share gratitude in text, but our experience shows that it tends to have more impact on the recipient when there is a human face and human voice with it.

5. Make sure everyone actually sees and hears the thanks they received.

Marica Rizzo

Community Manager
Acumen

Marica Rizzo is a community manager at Acumen, which is a global nonprofit tackling poverty with social entrepreneurship. Marica uses rituals as a way to reinforce culture when team members are far apart. She believes rituals can remind people where they are, emotionally and mentally, when they meet each other.

Work on Rituals

Part of her work was already virtual before the COVID-19 pandemic. She has been using rituals to build connection and trust among staff members and fellowship participants across different countries. She characterizes her organization's culture as a culture of reflection. Every meeting begins and ends with a reflective ritual. She sees rituals like bookends in opening and closing meetings. They act as containers. Rituals help protect the meetings

from ping-pong, email, Slack messages, and whatever else might be going on. Rituals honor people's moments of togetherness.

Learnings and Impact

Marica learned how important it is to close meetings with an a-ha or a reflection. It helps reinforce their identity as staff, as community members, as teammates. She also discovered that part of their culture at Acumen is to be reflective practitioners. This is constantly balancing between being out in the world, acting, taking action to create change, and then reflecting on our actions as individual change agents and leaders.

She emphasizes that they care about seeing each other's faces and the communication that comes with that. When everything went virtual, they learned how to continue caring about each other through subtle rituals such as check-in questions. For instance, during a staff meeting, they will give a question prompt. And then people get sent into a breakout room and meet three new people that they likely never met before to have a personal conversation. These kinds of small conversations would not have happened if the staff meeting was done in person. The use of virtual breakout rooms enabled them to get to know each other in new ways.

They also don't necessarily copy and paste from what they would do in person. They start with the same intentions and design new ways using the strengths of virtual tools. A recent coaching ritual illustrates this well. Coaching is part of their fellowship training. Before COVID-19, each person tried out a facilitator role. In their most recent virtual training, they had the same exercise. This time around, they gave some participants characters to act out. Participants without roles turned off their videos and just observed. This was a new way of coaching and worked well with the given affordances.

Recommendations to Others

Marica suggests other community leaders reinforce their shared identity as a group if they really want people to feel "I belong here" rather than "I just work here." She also thinks that so much of an organization's culture is about giving cues. At Acumen, the emphasis is really on being reflective. The A-ha ritual helps them reinforce that reflective practice. Everyone shares how they are feeling at that moment. The collective share-out gives a blueprint of where the team stands mentally and emotionally. They also create shared spaces like channels on Slack for people to share out their personal lives. She sees these not for the sake of having fun or being cool, but for reinforcing the culture of inclusivity.

Expectations for the Future

Her hope is that the future brings better and faster connections with other people. She thinks it's easier to distrust in the virtual world. It would be great if we could create technology that will help people to trust each other more. What's also exciting about distributed work is how many other cultures people get exposed to. This might influence people to become more inclusive. There's an absence of love when there's an unknown. As people become more connected, they will start to see that people have the capacity to be more.

5

Rituals for Focus, Engagement, and Flow

When People Are Spacing Out

When you need to center people's attention,
and make sure they are present for the meeting,
these rituals can increase their engagement.
They tap into people's senses and increase their
sense of intentionality by using words and
gestures deliberately.

"Enjoyment appears at the boundary between boredom and anxiety, when the challenges are just balanced with the person's capacity to act."
— Mihaly Csikszentmihalyi

Have you ever organized a meeting that just felt ... discombobulated? You had great intentions ... perhaps even high hopes. But as the meeting unfolded, things never got untracked, never hit a stride, never got into a rhythm. People ... spaced ... out ...

What if there were ways to get and keep meeting participants on the same page? What if there were ways to channel and direct our collective energy?

The rituals in Chapter 5 can provide a path. Choose rituals that work for your specific contexts and situations. Adopt and adapt rituals as you see fit.

Soundscape helps us sense what surrounds us as a group. **For All to See** allows people to quickly refer back to the ground we've travelled. **The Optimist Mirror** helps us synchronize like theatrical actors. **Perspective Pause** keeps a pulse on each other as we get through challenging material. **Curiosity Timeout** refocuses with participants' priorities. **Conductor's Wand** gets a team into a rehearsal mindset like a musical group. **Background Together** helps us feel together in a visual way. **Virtual Etiquette Guide** can avert the awkwardness you most dread.

8 Rituals for Focus, Engagement, and Flow

01 Soundscape
Sense Our Collective "Surroundings"

02 For All to See
Have a Magic Rewind Available

03 The Optimist Mirror
Synchronizing People in the Group to Act Together

04 Perspective Pause
Try to See It My Way / I'll Try to See It Your Way

05 Curiosity Timeout
Shift Wandering to Wondering

06 Conductor's Wand
Strategize Rehearsals for Successful Meetings

07 Background Together
Have Each Other's Back(ground)

08 Virtual Etiquette Guide
It's All About Avoiding Awkwardness

01 Soundscape

Moment

When a group can use a short mental break in a meeting, perhaps between agenda items or in the middle of a long agenda item.

This ritual can be done with a **group of any size.**

Intention

Create a space where people can momentarily shift their focus while also getting a sense of the collective "surroundings" of the group.

Time & Effort

Takes 60–90 seconds.

What is the ritual?

Soundscape can be a refocusing interlude between agenda items in a meeting. It can also be used as an opening warm-up.

The idea is simple. Take a short break where everyone unmutes their mics, closes their eyes, and listens for 30 seconds. No one talks. Since everyone's mic is unmuted, what we end up hearing is our collective soundscape, and the group is nudged to think about the distributed space we are in together.

Backstory

Glenn developed this ritual while leading the Borderless Fellowship for Justice Innovation, a program of the Thailand Institute of Justice, which is an affiliate of the United Nations. This fellowship brought together 11 young justice innovators from 10 countries across 4 continents.

Glenn noticed that the group could get some sense of their collective visual space by looking around the Gallery View in Zoom. However, it was more difficult to get a sense of the group's collective sonic space because several people would be on mute most of the time. (For example, one fellow would often participate from a noisy Internet cafe that had decent bandwidth.) So Glenn created a ritual to nudge people to notice the collective sonic space we were in together across the world.

How it works

1. "We're going to take a minute to get a sense of each other's space with a simple exercise."

2. "I'd like to ask everyone to unmute your mics. Don't worry if there are any background noises. We want to hear whatever it is you're hearing."

3. "Keep your video on, but please close your eyes."

4. "Now we're going to not say anything for 30 seconds, and just listen to what we hear."

5. [after 30 seconds] "Thanks for listening. What we just experienced is our collective soundscape."

02 For All to See

Moment

During a meeting where it's helpful to remember all the useful ideas that were raised.

This ritual can be done with a **group of any size.**

Intention

Absorb and get inspired by what's said in a meeting.

Time & Effort

Takes 1 minute to introduce at the beginning of the meeting and 1–2 minutes to share nuggets at the end. The primary notetaker works throughout the meeting.

What is the ritual?

It's difficult to remember all the key points and good ideas that were brought up in a meeting. So imagine if everyone in your meeting could mentally rewind and easily find an idea that someone mentioned earlier in the meeting.

Such magic exists. It's called "notes." :) However, many people aren't able to fully pay attention to people talking *and* take detailed notes at the same time.

For All to See is a ritual that combines collaborative note-taking with prompts at the end to notice and appreciate contributions.

Backstory

This ritual was inspired by seeing and hearing about different people's practices around collaborative note-taking, such as Brielle Harbin's methods at the United States Naval Academy. We were also inspired by Kemmon Guadeloupe's approach, which includes the use of prompts at the end of the meeting.

How it works

1. Designate one person who will have primary responsibility for taking notes that everyone will see. Notes can be taken in a digital space such as a Google Doc or a digital whiteboard such as MURAL.

2. At the start of the meeting, send a link to all participants for the digital space where notes are being captured. Encourage people to refer to it throughout the meeting.

3. During the meeting, the primary note-taker takes notes in the digital space, including who said what. The meeting facilitator periodically encourages participants to take a look at the notes.
    - The notes should be a concise summary that captures the gist of what was said. The notes should not look like a transcript.
    - Consider adding visual elements to the notes, such as icons, emoji, and simple drawings. You may also want to take screenshots of the video call to paste into the notes.

4. At the end of the meeting, the facilitator asks everyone take one last quick look at the notes, and find one useful nugget. Participants are asked to share nuggets from the notes. You can share nuggets verbally or through chat, depending on the size and the style of the group.

03 The Optimist Mirror

Moment

When a group is about to work on a task together, and needs a sync.

This is a **one-to-one ritual, will work up to four people.**

Intention

Synchronize people mentally, emotionally, and spark togetherness.

Time & Effort

Takes 5–10 minutes with quick debrief.

What is the ritual?

The Optimist Mirror is a ritual with small acts of movements that teammates perform face-to-face together to synchronize with each other. It's adapted from a well-known theatrical exercise to warm-up actors and actresses before acting. The ritual has three rounds where teammates explicitly alternate between leading and following. Following an external cue, the teammates enter a period of co-creating a mirror, by performing synchronized motions together. The Optimist Mirror can be used before a collaborative task where teammates need to be attentive, concentrated, and tuned in with each other.

Backstory

The inspiration for this ritual came from our conversation with Professor Lior Noy, a performance artist turned computational neuroscientist. Lior is fascinated by the effects of the mirror game in theater, and researched how it creates a sense of togetherness (Noy, 2014).

In one of his experiments, he worked with expert artists and novices. He measured how they move together. He discovered moments of togetherness happen when two improvisers let go of their reactive thinking and trust their moving together.

His research gives foundation to a phenomenon that happens to teams that work in synchrony. Lior also mentions how a similar kind of synchronization happens among jazz musicians and sports players.

How it works

1. Pair up your teammates and assign a breakout room for each pair.

2. Give them the instructions that there are three rounds of Optimist Mirror. In the first round they alternate movements in free flow, whereas in the second and third rounds they move together with a prompt.

3. First round is a warm-up round. It begins with short periods in which the players explicitly alternate between leading and following each other's movements.

4. Second round: Person A acts out an external cue: "It's a bright day." Person B follows person A, mimics her movements.

5. Third round: Person B acts out an external prompt: "It's a wonderful thing." Person A follows Person B, mimics her movements.

6. Closing, the pair picks a moment that they both like and perform it to the broader group.

04 Perspective Pause

Moment

At the beginning of a meeting topic where it would really help if participants were able to empathize with each other on the issue at hand.

This is a **small group ritual**.

Intention

Understand and keep in mind where everyone is coming from.

Time & Effort

Takes 5–7 minutes.

What is the ritual?

Sometimes, we could all use a reminder to try to see the world through another person's eyes. "Perspective taking" is the act of trying to understand a situation from another person's point of view, to take on their perspective. But just imagining another person's perspective is not enough.

Perspective Pause can help you and your colleagues be more consistent about empathizing with each other's point of view by prompting you to consider each other's possible perspectives, formulate questions, and eventually test your understanding of each other.

Backstory

This ritual was designed by Glenn as an exploration into perspective taking and a critique of perspective taking.

In theory, the idea of taking on another person's point of view seems very appealing as a vehicle for developing empathy with another person.

However, psychologist Nicholas Epley has empirically shown that simply imagining another person's point of view is not particularly effective. We tend not to be accurate based on imagination alone, and there's a real danger that we will overestimate how well we understand someone else (Epley, 2014).

This ritual is designed to start with guesses about other people's point of view, which can lead to curiosity, which can then spark questions we can ask to better understand their perspective. Glenn also borrows the "most charitable explanation" prompt from Kal Joffres' polar twins exercise in a class they co-taught.

How it works

1. This ritual is particularly useful at meetings where there are different and seemingly conflicting points of view on significant issues.

2. At either the beginning of the meeting, or at the beginning of the meeting agenda item that has significant differences, tell the group: "We're about to get into an important issue where understanding each other's perspective would be helpful, so we're going to take 5 minutes for a Perspective Pause."

3. "This is a silent exercise where each of us reflects so we can ask each other better questions in the rest of this meeting. Silently write notes to yourselves on:
    -   What would you guess is each person's perspective on this issue?
    -   What are the most charitable explanations for what you would guess is each person's perspective? Assume good intent.
    -   Treat your guesses as hypotheses. How might you test your hypotheses in this meeting? What questions might you ask each person during the meeting or after the meeting?
    -   We'll take 5 minutes to silently reflect and write down notes for ourselves."

05 Curiosity Timeout

Moment

When it feels like a significant chunk of the meeting attendees are getting mentally checked out of the meeting.

This can work both in **small and large groups**.

Intention

Refocus on what people want to learn from this particular meeting.

Time & Effort

Under 10 minutes depending on the size of the meeting.

What is the ritual?

Sometimes in a meeting, especially in a virtual meeting, people will mentally check out. To get people re-engaged, it can help to nudge their curiosity.

Curiosity Timeout is a short ritual you can use to focus meeting participants on what they want to learn from the meeting. While staying grounded in the purpose of the meeting, participants are invited to think about at least one thing they are curious about and then share that with the group.

Backstory

Glenn spontaneously created this ritual in a long, all-day meeting he was facilitating. About an hour after lunch ended, participants were hitting a major food coma, and some people also seemed to have their heads in other spaces, such as catching up on email.

Glenn called a timeout, and his first thought was to do something to tap into every participant's curiosity, and reset expectations so that their curiosity was more clearly connected to what was happening in the meeting.

How it works

1. The facilitator leads the activity: "I understand we all have a lot of things going on, a lot of things on our minds. Let's take a quick Curiosity Timeout to refocus on this meeting."

2. "Given that the purpose of this meeting is _____, what's one thing that you are curious about?"

3. "Take 20 seconds to think about it."

4. "Now let's share ..." Sharing can be done verbally for smaller groups, and via the chat in videoconferencing for larger groups.

5. The facilitator quickly reviews what has been shared, and summarizes which topics will be addressed in this meeting, and how those that won't be addressed in this meeting can be addressed in other forums.

06 Conductor's Wand

Moment

Before a major milestone or the end of a project or event.

This is a **small group ritual**.

Intention

Get ready for a major meeting.

Time & Effort

Under 10 minutes, low effort.

What is the ritual?

Conductor's Wand, a beautiful rehearsal, is a ritual to help a team to get into a rehearsal mindset. It primes a team to focus on the essential elements of a meeting rehearsal such as transitions.

Virtual meetings require extra care due to the limitations of cues in the virtual space. When team members cannot easily read each other's cues, they cannot respond to unexpected turns in a meeting. This makes rehearsals a must, especially for high-stakes meetings. Teams can apply this ritual at the beginning of their rehearsal to improve its effectiveness.

Backstory

The inspiration for this ritual came from our conversation with J. P. Stephens, an organizational behavior professor at Case Western University. J. P. Stephens's research looks at how high-performing teams such as a choir or a construction crew coordinate their actions. J. P. did extensive fieldwork by attending choir rehearsals (Stephens, 2014).

His research shows two things regarding rehearsals that we can bring to virtual meetings. J. P. discovered that rehearsals are where the conductor and choir members deliberately work on transitions between different sound groups. When things begin to fall apart, choir members need to respond to them in milliseconds. The conductor helps in those moments to course-correct, to get back to her perception of a beautiful sound. Similar to a choir, a meeting can leverage a conductor role to define the quality of a meeting, and master the coordination between team members.

During rehearsals, choir members gain mastery at distributing their attention between themselves, their counterparts, and the conductor. They constantly switch between the questions of: What am I doing? What are other people doing? What's the conductor doing? What's in my score? By spreading their attention across all the different resources in their environment, they learn how to knit those back together again. This adaptive attention can be leveraged during virtual meeting rehearsals.

How it works

1. Give a heads-up to the team that there is a ritual before the rehearsal.

2. Introduce Conductor's Wand. Conductor's Wand helps you discover what transitions and other critical parts of the meeting you need to rehearse.

3. Open up a virtual whiteboard and invite everyone.

4. Brainstorm all the transitions that need rehearsal, and all the things that can go wrong in the actual meeting.

   Prompt 1: Transition between speakers (Person A to Person B)

   Prompt 2: Transition between tools (Zoom, slides, virtual whiteboard, screen share)

   Prompt 3: Transition between content topics (from discovery to design)

5. Now discuss about the energy arc of the meeting. Where are possible fall-outs? (e.g. right after a 10-minute presentation)

6. If there's a long list and time crunch, vote for the most critical ones to rehearse. If there's plenty of time, commit to rehearsing all of the transitions.

7. Start your rehearsal.

07 Background Together

Moment
At the start of a meeting or start of a specific agenda item.

This ritual can be done with a **group of any size.**

Intention
Unify and focus

Time & Effort
This can take as little as 5 minutes to create and organize, but it can get as elaborate as you'd like!

What is the ritual?

Imagine you had an easy way of creating a bit of camaraderie and esprit de corps with some or all of your meeting participants. It's like everyone wearing the same custom t-shirt, without having to worry about clothing sizes.

Background Together is a way to feel a sense of shared identity using virtual backgrounds, a feature available in many videoconferencing applications.

The general idea is to find or create virtual backgrounds that express something around your team's identity, purpose, goals, or roles. The backgrounds can be the exact same for everyone or can be a set of backgrounds based on a theme.

Backstory

We've seen people use virtual backgrounds in many different organizations and teams. For example, at virtual gatherings of the entire teaching community of the Stanford d.school, with around 50 people showing up, the core Teaching & Learning Team of 5 to 6 people all have the same background so that people know who's organizing and available to help.

A very different example is the "real background trading" of some people at MURAL. Person A takes a of photo of their physical room, then Person B uses that photo as their virtual background and vice versa. This creates a sense of being in each other's spaces.

How it works

1. There are different ways you can find or create virtual backgrounds:
   - You can find virtual backgrounds on the Internet (e.g. try searching for: free virtual background images).
   - You can create a custom background using a photo you have taken.
   - You can create a custom background by creating a slide in Google Slides or PowerPoint exporting that slide as an image file – and with slides, it's easy to add both images and text.

2. In advance of your meeting:
   - Decide who is going to find or create the background. You might have one person responsible, or it can be a collaborative effort with 2 or 3 people.
   - Brainstorm several different ideas of what you might want the background to convey. Pick your favorite idea.
   - Find or create the background.
   - Distribute the background to the people who will be using it during the meeting.

3. During the meeting:
   - Have the appropriate people use the background at the appropriate time.
   - The background might be used for the entire meeting, or it could be used for specific parts of the meeting. It depends on what you want the background to accomplish.

WE ARE GOING TO DO AN ACTIVITY TO AVOID SOCIAL AWKWARDNESS...

VIRTUAL ETIQUETTE GUIDE

LET'S QUICKLY SHARE, WHAT DO YOU FIND AWKWARD IN OUR VIRTUAL MEETINGS?

START OF A MEETING

WHEN PEOPLE ARE ON MUTE & YOU TRY TO TELL THEM BY SHOWING YOUR EARS

HOW TO AVOID THAT? MAYBE WHENEVER YOU TALK CHECK IF THE MIC IS ON

LIKE YOU'RE AN ANCHOR WOMAN

08 Virtual Etiquette Guide

Moment

As a team, working group, or committee is starting to work together and wants its group interactions to feel smoother.

This ritual can be done with a **group of any size.**

Intention

Be courteous to each other.

Time & Effort

Under 20 minutes, depends on the size of the group.

What is the ritual?

Etiquette gets a bad rap in some circles. It does have a classist history, largely existing to protect the social standing of elites and help them avoid various faux pas. (After all, etiquette originally meant "keep off the grass" during the time of Louis XIV.)

Let's reframe etiquette to mean: "stuff we all do to avoid social awkwardness and make each other feel more comfortable."

In Virtual Etiquette Guide, your group identifies socially awkward pain points they want to avoid, and agrees on what everyone will do to eliminate or reduce the awkwardness.

Backstory

Virtual Etiquette Guide has its roots in meeting facilitation practices such as ground rules and community agreements. But the feel of Virtual Etiquette Guide is lighter and more irreverent, as it's primarily about avoiding social awkwardness.

How it works

1. This ritual can be valuable for a group that meets on a regular basis. At one of your meetings, allocate 15 minutes for this activity. It's a modest investment of time that will have benefits for all future meetings of the group.
2. Frame it in a fun way for the group: "We're going to do an activity to AVOID SOCIAL AWKWARDNESS. After all, who wants to be awkward?? The activity is called 'Virtual Etiquette Guide.'"
3. Solicit the pains of the group: "Let's quickly share, what do you find awkward in a virtual meeting? It could be something *painfully* awkward. Or just, 'Um ... awkward!'" Depending on group size you can ask people to share out loud, in chat, or in a shared Google Doc or MURAL.
4. Affirm the awkwardness. As people share what they find awkward, say things like, "Yikes, that *can* be awkward!"
5. After you put together an "awkward list," for each item, suggest a practice that could mitigate the awkwardness. For example:

Awkward	Awkward Mitigators
+ Start of meeting.	+ Meetings begin no later than 2 minutes of the scheduled time. + Have a silent activity that people can do as others are joining the meeting – perhaps it's a question to mull on or write a few thoughts on.
+ I have a question, how do I ask it?	+ There are lots of options most important thing is to agree on which method(s) you will use. Options include: a) say out loud "I have a question," b) put the question in chat, c) use the Raise Hand functionality in Zoom.
+ How to prevent meetings from running over time.	+ Have someone screen-share a countdown timer when there are less than 5 minutes remaining.

J. P. Stephens

Associate Professor of Organizational Behavior at Case Western Reserve University - Weatherhead School of Management

Work on High-Performing Groups

J. P. Stephens is an organizational behavior scientist who studies responsiveness in groups. In his research, he looks at how experts in group settings coordinate with each other while they are performing high-skill tasks. He has done fieldwork with choirs and construction crews. He has discovered key insights that can inspire rituals for virtual meetings.

In his fieldwork with a choir, he was both a bass singer and a researcher. As he attended rehearsals, he also observed and interviewed 35 choir members. He found that a conductor who makes the group go through deliberate practice is critical in the success of the collective. During rehearsals, individuals learn how to become a high-performing group that is unified around a common goal. In his fieldwork with a construction crew, J. P. found a very

similar rehearsal mindset. Deliberate practice of a high-stakes meeting before the actual meeting can apply to virtual meetings.

His research revealed more about the "how" of rehearsals as well. Choral musical performances can be quite long at 2–3 hours. During a rehearsal, the group doesn't have the luxury to rehearse everything. It's the conductor's role to strategize and identify areas where the group is falling behind. The conductor then focuses on improving those challenging parts with the group, one part at a time.

Ways Toward a Beautiful Meeting

His fieldwork helped J. P. discover the relationship between group performance and aesthetics of a meeting. During a rehearsal, the conductor leads the ensemble of musicians based on her or his perception of beauty.

This notion of beauty is like a north star. The conductor sets the threshold for what's beautiful musically and what's not, and shows the path for the group based on that beauty standard. When it comes to virtual meetings, J. P. sees four things that can help the meeting host toward a beautiful meeting: 1) having a sense of the whole; 2) a sense of clarity in roles and agenda; 3) a sense of smoothness; and 4) an adaptive mindset.

Beauty is about experiencing a sense of the whole. In virtual meetings, this can require a lot of effort. One way to tackle this is to have smaller-sized meetings. For instance, J. P. recently heard from colleagues that they are looking forward to a smaller-sized class experience so they can see the entire class together. He says, "the felt sense of the whole gets fragmented when it's not clear who's in the room, and who's speaking in Gallery View."

Providing a sense of clarity in goals, roles, and flow of the meeting can also help toward a beautiful meeting. There's a strong body of research that found having and following an agenda increases meeting satisfaction. J. P. says, "Having a clear sense of the work ahead, maintaining clear time boundaries for agenda sections, and explicitly marking that each item has been 'closed' in a certain way will help."

J. P. suggests working toward a sense of smoothness in virtual meetings by setting clear ground rules and signaling participation. The meeting chair can co-create these rules with participants and reinforce them. For instance, people can use the "raise hand" feature as well as mute until it's their turn to speak.

Lastly, J. P. emphasizes the importance of an adaptive and resilient mindset in the face of breakdowns based on his work on choral singing. He says, "If someone's audio signal conks out altogether, each individual running the meeting needs to have the capability to flexibly repair. The meeting chair should be aware of the affordances of the technology and be able to advise folks, as well as keep the meeting flowing. Honoring participants' expectations and respecting their time should contribute to a sense of a beautiful meeting."

Expectations for the Future

J. P. is excited about the changing landscape of work. The future will be more diverse with people working from home, working from an office, and in between. J. P. thinks this "may usher in a 'cyborg' age of connectivity, if you will, where human affectivity has to be communicated both physically and virtually when we meet and where, in a given organization, some individuals will be physically connecting and others virtually connecting." He's also excited as a researcher to have easy access to data to understand how and why we connect, since we can easily record virtual meetings.

6

Rituals for Resilience and Rejuvenation

Combating "Zoom Fatigue"

These rituals can balance out busy virtual meetings, by giving participants more mental and emotional space.
They can encourage people to pause, reflect, and refresh in the moment – as well as to set and reinforce boundaries for themselves.

"Shutting off the thought process is not rejuvenating; the mind is like a car battery – it recharges by running." – Bill Watterson

During the COVID-19 pandemic in 2020, we heard about "Zoom fatigue" so much, that we were starting to get fatigued from hearing about Zoom fatigue. Ugh!

The pain was palpable, but it begged the question: What could be done in our lives today? Taking breaks from your computer and periodically substituting phone calls for video calls help, but what else can be done to rejuvenate and resile in an increasingly virtual world?

The rituals in Chapter 6 can serve as a start. **Olympic Workout** channels your sports hero. **New Sensation** gets us feeling together – whoa! **Variety Hour** has us share what we care about. **Virtual Charades** gets us guessing. **Personal Tour** takes us through each other's spaces. **Around the World in 60 Minutes** transports us to new destinations. **Serendipity Scavenger Hunt** fosters social interactions outside of formal meetings. **Walk and Talk** has us move while we meet.

8 Rituals for Resilience and Rejuvenation

01 Olympic Workout
Set the Energy Level at the Beginning of a Meeting

02 New Sensation
Feel It Together to Get in the Same Space

03 The Variety Hour
Share Your Work and Passion Projects

04 Virtual Charades
Get People Comfortable with Putting Their Ideas Forward

05 Personal Tour
Take a Walk Through Each Other's Space

06 Around the World in 60 Minutes
Explore New Destinations Together

07 Serendipity Scavenger Hunt
Encourage Casual Collisions

08 Walk and Talk
Move to Find a Groove

01 Olympic Workout

Moment
During a meeting where the energy level is low.

This can work in **small and large groups.**

Intention
Express gratitude for each other.

Time & Effort
Under 5 minutes, low effort.

What is the ritual?

Olympic Workout is a quick, high-intensity-interval-training ritual. The ritual involves selecting a super athlete, followed by several 30-second, long-proven exercises that boost people's energy level.

Physical exercise has a direct influence on people's moods and energy level. Research in sports illustrates that even small bursts of physical activity can improve people's well-being (Tabata et al., 1996). There is, however, a barrier to working out, given the busyness of worklife, lack of motivation, and lack of habit. Olympic Workout aims to nudge people toward exercising by introducing aspirational sports figures.

Backstory

This ritual takes its inspiration from micro-workouts and a superhero exercise.

Micro-workouts, also known as high-intensity-interval-training (HIIT), consist of several sets of short bursts of exercise, followed by a rest period. We came across embedding this kind of physical exercising into meetings at IDEO Chicago. They use yoga, pilates, planks, and HIITS in their meetings. Physical exercises can also be a stand-alone session as shown in our connection rituals by Atölye from Istanbul, and students from Stanford Graduate School of Business.

The superhero exercise by Ayse Birsel is a simple exercise to motivate people to discover their values and aspirations. You pick a superhero in your life and imagine yourself as that superhero. Then you identify values of that superhero as your own, and aspire to live by those values.

How it works

1. Pick an athlete or sports hero. If you are short of ideas, pick one on the list.
    *   Michael Phelps
    *   Serena Williams
    *   LeBron James

2. Now you are that athlete, getting ready for your daily practice.

3. Start your micro-workout with 10 squats.

4. Continue with 10 jumping jacks.

5. Finish up with a 30-second plank.

02 New Sensation

Moment

When you want to get into the same space together – can be at the start of a meeting, a transition in the middle, or at the end.

This is a **small group ritual** that can be adjusted to a large group.

Intention

Sync up and energize together.

Time & Effort

Can take as little as 1 minute to do in a meeting.

What is the ritual?

Experiencing a physical sensation together can help us feel together. For example, there's something about feeling that first downhill when riding a roller coaster together. Or there's something about prepping food together, whether it's assembling sandwiches or wrapping egg rolls.

New Sensation is a ritual to help us create a physical sensation that we experience together when we're in different places. We'll explain it here using an example of ice water, but you can experiment with different sensations that generate a distinct impression. :)

Backstory

Glenn developed New Sensation as a Creative Stretch for the Stanford d. school stories on Instagram. His point of departure in developing the ritual was to explore how we might activate our sense of touch together in a virtual meeting, but it could be used for other senses as well.

How it works

1. Choose a physical sensation that everyone in the meeting can create where they are.
    - Make sure the sensation is something that people will clearly feel, and one that everyone can feel at roughly the same time, one that kicks in relatively quickly.
    - A good starter sensation is putting your hand into a bowl of ice water!

2. Before the meeting, let meeting participants know what they will need to have in hand (e.g. a bowl of ice water).

3. During the meeting, when you want to create a syncing moment, guide the group through New Sensation with instructions such as: "Before we get into the next item, we're going to take a moment to experience a new sensation. At the count of 3, put your hand in your bowl of ice water, and keep it there for 20 seconds."

4. People will see, hear, and feel each other's reactions. No instructions necessary for this step. :)

03 The Variety Hour

Moment
Whenever you want to share content — personal and professional — in an engaging way.

This ritual can be done by a **group of any size.**

Intention
Discover where teammates get their energy (from side projects to customer engagements).

Time & Effort
High in planning. The actual event can be 30–60 minutes.

What is the ritual?

The Variety Hour is a ritual designed to encourage team members to share their work and passions with the community. People sign up for sessions that are anywhere from 1–30 minutes long, and share whatever content they want — either personal or professional. This gives people the freedom to share things they care about and helps coworkers discover where their team-mates get their energy from.

The inaugural Variety Hour had a spectrum of share-outs: There were serious project stories, a 1-minute group screaming session about the pandemic, a 3-minute segment called "Nom Nom Nope" where a colleague fed goats various foods and the audience had to guess whether they'd find them delicious or disgusting, and a 5-minute dance party, among other inspiring shares.

Backstory

The Variety Hour comes from IDEO Chicago. Annette Ferrara, one the workplace experience directors, and a team of designers created a new initiative called The Summer of Serendipity to help team members strengthen relationships by learning from each other. The team received feedback that the randomness and creativity of this virtual event felt most like the vibe of being in a physical studio together. This ritual emerged in a grassroots and organic way. A group of designers and directors just began to get together virtually to talk about the current ways they share and do creative things, and what they could try that's new or different. Working remotely, they recognized they were missing moments to see and share work, connect, and strengthen their relationships and community by learning and sharing with each other. Many of these moments used to happen spontaneously, while getting a cup of coffee in the kitchen or walking by a project room.

How it works

1. Set a Variety Hour in your organization's calendar.

2. Invite people to share whatever they want to share during the session. This is an anything-goes moment and a time to shine and share – think community theater – so encourage the community to come as they are.

3. Line up the presenters beforehand and make sure to work out all technical issues and rehearse transitions between share-outs.

4. During the Variety Hour, encourage people to turn on their videos and come off mute to provide spontaneous feedback.

5. After the Variety Hour, run a feedback survey, and get the pulse of the audience for the next session.

04 Virtual Charades

Moment

At a major milestone or the end of a project or event.

This is a **small group ritual.**

Intention

Express gratitude for each other.

Time & Effort

Low effort in planning. Actual ritual can be 10 minutes or less, can be extended.

What is the ritual?

Virtual Charades is a guessing game for movies, book names, or songs. Teammates pair up. One of them picks a movie and sends a direct message to their partner. The partner needs to act out the title by using gestures and movements without using any words. The winner pair is the one with the highest number of right guesses.

Dana Nau describes charades as a game of pantomimes (Nau, 2000). You need to act out a title of a book, movie, play, song, or tv show without speaking, while the other people in the group try to guess the title. The objective is to guess the title as quickly as possible.

Backstory

Charades is a well-known game for social gatherings. Laïla von Alvensleben has been running the virtual version of charades as meeting energizers in her work at MURAL. She finds energizers great for refocusing attention and increasing engagement. They can be done at any time when the meeting facilitator senses a need for an energy boost. Energizers need to be fast-paced and positive, leaving people in an elevated mood, and motivated to engage with others.

How it works

1. Pair each participant with someone else.

2. Ask each person to choose a title of a book, movie, play, TV show, or song that their partner will have to imitate in front of the webcam to the rest of the group.

3. Tell participants to send the title they chose in a direct message to their partner.

4. In pairs, take turns acting out what your partner sent you. The rest of the group has 1 minute to guess what you're mimicking.

Professor Nau gives some verbal instructions you can give on how to effectively act out titles.

- Book title: "Unfold your hands as if they were a book."

- Movie title: "Pretend to crank an old-fashioned movie camera."

- Play title: "Pretend to pull the rope that opens a theater curtain."

- Song title: "Pretend to sing."

- TV show: "Draw a rectangle to outline the TV screen."

05 Personal Tour

Moment

When team members need
to connect at human level.

Intention

Show a glimpse of personal
life.

This is a **small group ritual,** but can
be adjusted to large groups.

Time & Effort

Can be as quick as 1 minute per
person sharing. Or you could elect
to take more leisurely tours.

What is the ritual?

Personal Tour is a quick and fun way to get a more three-dimensional sense
of the spaces that each of us is in.

It's best done with people joining a video call on their phone so that they can
freely move around. The idea is simple – give us a walking tour of the space
you are in.

One important caveat: Make sure that people on your call are comfortable
with sharing a view of a part of their physical space on screen. (See "How it
works" section, IMPORTANT NOTE, for variations.)

Backstory

Personal Tours originated in the Stanford d.school's Design Across Borders class during the Autumn 2017 quarter. Half of the students were at the d. school, and the other half were 8,000 miles away at TCDC (Thailand Creative & Design Center) in Bangkok. One of the ways in which international team-mates got to know each other better was to take each other on Personal Tours of their buildings.

How it works

1. Have people join a video call on their phone.

2. If your group is larger than six people, consider sending people into breakout rooms to do this ritual in small groups.

3. Take turns giving each other tours of each other's spaces, with people walking through a space and explaining what you are seeing. (e.g. "This is the kitchen, and here's where I make my coffee ... ")
    *   TIP: If you are on a video call on your phone, you can switch from the front camera to the back camera. It will be easier to walk through a space, plus you will give people a point-of-view shot of your space.

IMPORTANT NOTE:
Make sure that people are comfortable showing their physical space to everyone on the call. People might not want others to see parts of their "messy place," or there might be other people in the space whose privacy might be intruded on. Someone may elect to limit the tour to a certain part of their space. Or another alternative is for a person to go outside and show what they see outside their place.

06 Around the World in 60 Minutes

Moment
When sense of time loses its meaning, and depression kicks in.

This is a **small group ritual**.

Intention
Make memories so that there is variety and more positive emotions.

Time & Effort
It requires planning. The actual ritual can be 30–60 minutes.

What is the ritual?

Around the World in 60 minutes is a virtual journey where team members pick an exotic destination and explore the highlights of the destination together through wandering around via Google Earth, sightseeing via video clips, dancing to its music, and enjoying the food by everyone ordering the cuisine specialties from the destination.

The passage of time is harder to discern in virtual meetings because we tend not to change our surroundings. People can feel like every day and every meeting is the same, like in the movie *Groundhog Day*.

To make things memorable, create more variability in virtual interactions. Around the World in 60 minutes makes collective memories and sparks positive feelings amongst team members.

Backstory

This ritual was inspired by Jules Verne's *80 Days Around the World* and the show *Amazing Race*. Kursat began a new ritual with his family after the shelter-in-place in the U.S. They watched *Amazing Race* every night to lighten the heaviness of lockdown. If people cannot go anywhere, they can at least imagine being in those locations. A UCL psychologist Dr. Julia Shaw, author of *The Memory Illusion*, has a similar ritual of picking a location and taking a virtual trip across the world with her partner. She calls out these virtual trip nights as temporal landmarks where they can remember and celebrate the passage of time (McRobbie, 2020).

How it works

1. Pick a destination together as a team. You can make this a fun activity by finding images from exotic destinations and voting on them together.

2. Once you identify the destination, the next thing to do is to form your crew, like Mr. Fogg in the story. There are three guides: Travel Guide, Culinary Guru, and a Music Guru.

3. Guides work on the content. For instance, select a dish and do a group food order for every team member, or select a video to watch together, music to listen to, etc.

4. During the journey in the meeting, make sure to change your virtual background and take a group picture like you would do when you visit a landmark in that destination.

5. Close the meeting with music, a bit of chit-chat on impressions, and even dance.

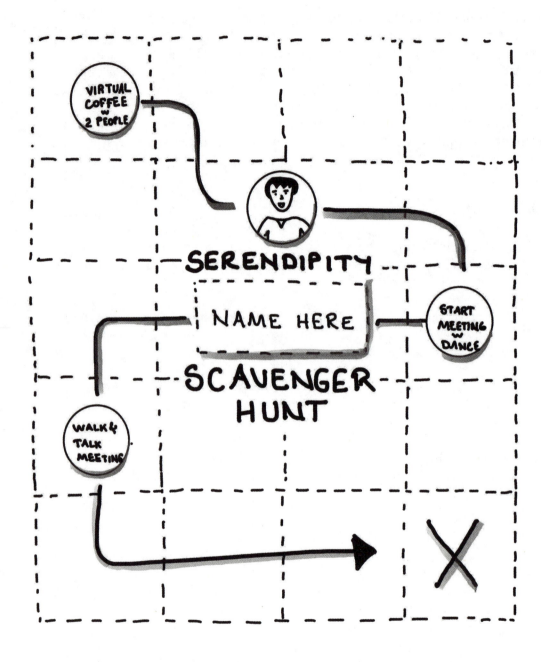

07 Serendipity Scavenger Hunt

Moment

Whenever you notice people are falling into predictable ruts or inter-acting with the same people all the time.

This is a **large group ritual.**

Intention

Encourage casual collisions between coworkers, strengthen "weak ties" between community members, foster an inclusive culture, and introduce more serendipity and spontaneity into remote work.

Time & Effort

High in preparation. You need a coordinator. The actual scavenger hunt is relatively high effort to complete the tasks.

What is the ritual?

Serendipity Scavenger Hunt is a game to encourage team members to meet each other outside of formal meetings. The intention is to strengthen rela-tionships in the community by creating serendipitous encounters.

The Scavenger Hunt is a constellation of smaller rituals such as walking meet-ings, virtual coffee times, impromptu stretching, and dance parties. Games can also include expressive acts like making a themed playlist for the team and inviting a pet, kid, or plant to Zoom-bomb a recurring meeting. The first person to complete the Scavenger Hunt gets a prize.

Backstory

The Serendipity Scavenger Hunt ritual was designed by Annette Ferrara and a team of designers at IDEO Chicago. They observed that the way most people held Zoom meetings was too formal and that serendipitous interactions they normally would have had passing each other in hallways or grabbing a snack in the kitchen were slowly eroding. To address this gap, the team designed a ritual to motivate people to create more opportunities to have serendipitous interactions.

How it works

1. Create a list of scavenger hunt activities, lay them out in a bingo card – like matrix in Google Slides. Feel free to use the ones below or come up with your own:
   - Slack 3 people whose status is "active" and you don't know well. Try an audio-only call via Slack. Go on a walking meeting. Start a meeting with stretching or an impromptu dance party. Invite a pet, kid, or plant to Zoom-bomb a recurring meeting. Start/end meetings with a themed song. Make a themed playlist for your team. Sign up for a virtual Meet n' Three (see the ritual in Chapter 9); Install the Donut app on Slack. Join standups early to make chit-chat. Have lunch with someone from a different discipline. Invite someone to join you for coffee over Zoom.

2. Start your scavenger hunt. Type your name on your card to claim it and copy your headshot "bingo chip" to use as your tokens. When you complete an activity, mark it with a bingo chip.

3. Post pictures proving you completed your activities into a dedicated Slack channel.

4. The first to fill out their whole card receives a randomly chosen gift from the organizer.

08 Walk and Talk

Moment
When you need to meet but want a break from sitting in front of a computer.

This is a **small group ritual.**

Intention
Change the dynamic of your conversation by being on the move.

Time & Effort
Unless you think walking is hard, this is easy! You'll be walking for however long your meeting is.

What is the ritual?

We can spend an inordinate amount of time sitting down in front of our computers when we are a distributed workforce, whether we are on video calls or doing other work. The irony is that with technology, often, we could be anywhere.

Walk and Talk involves exactly what you'd expect from its name – talking while walking. We add in occasional descriptions of each of our surroundings to help us get a sense of the collective physical spaces we are in.

Backstory

The Walk and Talk ritual is partly inspired by the walk and talks people will do in offices (e.g. in the hallway on the way to another meeting, or going outside to get a breath of fresh air, or getting a cup of coffee). But there are tweaks to account for the fact that we are in different places when we're distributed.

The core idea remains to walk while we talk.

How it works

1. Let your meeting attendees know in advance that your upcoming meeting will be a Walk and Talk.

    - Ask everyone to have their phone and headphones ready when the meeting starts.
    - Ask everyone to find a place they can walk while talking, preferably outside (parks are great!). Avoid loud places.

2. Hold your meeting over a conference call or over a videoconference with video off and everyone on their phones.

3. As the meeting starts, have everyone start walking wherever they are. Before you dive into the meeting agenda, to get sense of your collective set of places, have everyone briefly describe where they are, and three things they see where they are walking.

4. Throughout the meeting, perhaps every 10 minutes, have one person at random quickly describe what they are seeing where they are walking.

LAÏLA VON ALVENSLEBEN

Head of Culture and Collaboration at MURAL

Laïla Von Alvensleben is a remote work coach with a background in UX design. She uses rituals to grow and sustain a culture for a distributed organization with few co-located people. For Laïla, rituals are a way to emotionally connect with people and help them to discover their commonalities.

Her career started while she was working as a UX designer in a fully distributed product design team. As she grew into her remote work life, she researched and developed best practices on remote work. She takes her inspiration from her personal career trajectory and from her network of remote collaborators. Designing rituals for her starts with tuning into the existing culture of an organization and finding the threads to work with. Once tuned in, it's easier to find the weaknesses and strengths of the current culture. Strengths give you a base to build on; weaknesses give you the opportunities for improvement.

Work on Rituals

When it comes to the actual design of a ritual, she believes in the importance of experimentation. Before rolling out a ritual in an organization, she first tests her ideas with her close circle of friends and gauges the engagement and tests the overall flow. Once she's confident that the proposed ritual would work, she takes it to the meetings and gatherings of the medium-sized company she works for.

She has created a wide variety of rituals. Some of them are mini-interaction rituals, such as attaching a company value to a kudos while chatting with a colleague. Some of them are part of bigger rituals. For instance, she is responsible for crafting the company-wide all hands meetings. When she first started working on these, pain points were around length, monotony, and irregularity of the content. She opens up the meetings with warm-up activities to help participants loosen up. To break the monotony, she invites customers to tell their stories. These led to higher engagement and satisfaction.

Learnings and Impact

Laïla sees rituals and habits hand-in-hand with shaping culture. She learned in her work that most of the virtual culture is documented. Companies that are well known for their remote setups, such as Automattic and Buffer, have codified their culture in elaborate ways using Wiki. She sees this codification as a sign of maturity for nurturing culture online.

Recommendation to Others

She suggests starting with understanding the existing culture and identifying its strengths and weaknesses. Once you have that under your belt, involve leadership and facilitate a conversation around what to focus on. There needs to be a focus on broadening the conversation by involving the employees in a town hall meeting. Once there are actionable steps, workshop those steps toward implementation. This can be in the form of best practices, rituals, habits, and etiquette.

Expectations for the Future

She's curious about extended reality, the physical aspect of it as well as the intangible aspect of it. Extended reality is a broader term to cover augmented reality, virtual reality, and mixed reality. From a recent conversation with a friend, she learned about its potential power of altering a person's reality. She's skeptical about the promise of it, and not sure about getting excited about it, since there's an obvious dark side to it.

7

Rituals for Creating Connection and Building Relationships

Get to Know You: Build and Sustain Relationships

Use these rituals to improve how people connect during virtual meetings, by giving them cues to build empathy, learn more about each other, and foster trust for more meaningful relationships.

"Empathy ... is an offer of accompaniment and commitment. And making the offer changes you." – Sherry Turkle

Pause for a minute and reflect: Think about your colleagues with whom you've gotten the most done. With whom have you had the most productive and most fulfilling collaborations? We're willing to bet you had a pretty good relationship with them.

Relationships matter. And they can matter even more when you're collaborating virtually. Trust and care can go a long way when we're not in the same place. We want to feel understood as human beings.

What if we could build vibrant and strong relationships with each other while we were in different places? The rituals in Chapter 7 support your human connection efforts.

Road Trip fosters the kind of deeper conversations we have when traveling together. **Connection Web** weaves us together through gratitude. **Virtual High-Quality Connection** shows that meaningful connections don't need to take long to develop. **Smell Together** brings us closer with a shared scent. **Team Positivity Contagion** creates a series of positivity events. **You Never Would Have Guessed** lets us into each other's surprising secrets. **Conversation Cuts** changes how we pay attention and read the room. **Team Symbol** crystallizes a visual rallying point.

8 Rituals for Connection and Building Relationships

01 Road Trip
Travel and Talk While Enjoying the Scenery

02 Connection Web
Show Gratitude and Acknowledge Each Other

03 Virtual High-Quality Connection
Connect as People Before Jumping into Business

04 Smell Together
Create a Co-sensory Connection While Far Apart

05 Team Positivity Contagion
Create Positive Energy While Virtually Connecting

06 You Never Would Have Guessed
Surface a Surprising Secret

07 Conversation Cuts
How We Look at a Conversation

08 Team Symbol
Shared Identity with a Visual Symbol

01 Road Trip

Moment
When we want to have a deeper, more profound conversation.

This is a **1:1 ritual**.

Intention
Foster the feeling of being in a space together, side-by-side.

Time & Effort
Takes 3–5 minutes to find a video on the Internet that you can use as your road trip footage to screen share.

What is the ritual?

Think about where you've had some of your deepest conversations with people in any part of your life, whether in a personal or work context.

Many people experience some of their deepest conversations on road trips. There's something about the not-so-focused experience that helps us relax and open up. There's something about looking at the road ahead while talking with each other. We don't constantly look at each other in the face, but can look at each other occasionally. We also have the ambient sound of the road noise, and perhaps the car stereo.

In this ritual, we simulate the feeling of a road trip in a virtual meeting.

Backstory

This ritual was inspired by Mario Roset, the co-founder and CEO of Civic House, which helps strengthen and scale social impact start-ups in Latin America.

Mario noticed the conversation dynamics of his road trips, and started a weekly radio show where he goes on a one-hour virtual road trip with his guests, and the audience listens in through an online radio station. The conversations have been remarkably deep and revealing, and Mario continues to play with the format.

How it works

1. When you want to have a deeper conversation with someone in a virtual meeting, ask them if they would go on a (virtual) road trip with you. Let them know they don't need to do anything special other than show up for a video call.

2. Before the call starts, find some road trip video footage that you can screen share during the meeting. Go to YouTube, search for: road trip background. Pick a video you like.

3. When the call starts, start your road trip video footage and screen-share it. Consider including the sound in your screen share, and adjust the volume in YouTube so it's not too loud for the person you're talking with.

4. Have a conversation and enjoy the journey together.

   Variation: As an alternative to a road trip, try sitting at the waterfront together. Or a campfire. (Search for waterfront background or campfire background on YouTube.)

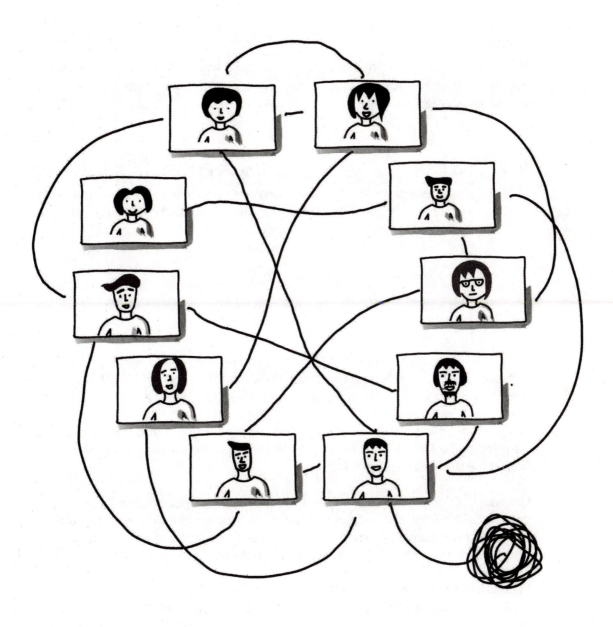

02 Connection Web

Moment

When people need to connect with their team members at the end of a meeting.

This is a **small group ritual,** but can be adjusted to large groups.

Intention

Show how connected we all are.

Time & Effort

Preparation of the slides will take 10–30 minutes. The actual ritual will depend on the size of the group. You can give 1–2 minutes per person.

What is the ritual?

The Connection Web, created by Acumen, started a ritual where team members would sit in a circle, and there would be a ball of yarn. Let's say Lisa is the first person with ball of yarn. Lisa wraps the yarn thread around her hand. She picks Stephanie as the next recipient and tosses the ball of yarn to her, When Stephanie has the ball of yarn, Lisa shares a thought about Stephanie. It could be something Lisa learned from Stephanie, or something about Stephanie that Lisa is grateful for.

Once Lisa is done, Stephanie tosses the ball of yarn to Pat, and the cycle continues. A person can receive the ball of yarn only once. At the end, when everyone has received the ball of yarn, there is a spider web effect and a visual representation of how connected people are.

When things went virtual, the Acumen team decided to adapt this ritual. They created a Google Slide, drew a large circle, and then got headshots of everyone in a circle. Instead of throwing a ball of yarn, Lisa would draw a line from her to Stephanie to symbolize the metaphorical yarn toss.

Backstory

Connection Web is adapted from an in-person ritual from the Acumen Fellowship Program. The initial version of the ritual happened at the end of an eight-week bootcamp and marked its closure. The ritual gave each participant the opportunity to share appreciation and gratitude for their cohort members.

When everything went virtual, Acumen wanted to keep the intention and feel of the ritual. The core idea is to have a moment of gratitude and acknowledge that people have formed bonds.They've developed a shared identity as a cohort of change agents.

Marica Rizzo, a facilitator who ran both physical and virtual versions of Connection Web, found the virtual version was as effective as the physical one. Both versions give a moment of acknowledgment for people in a world where most people are not well practiced at acknowledging each other. The ritual invites people to honor each other, one person at a time, in a group that has formed new bonds.

How it works

1. Create one slide in a Google Slides presentation. Insert a large circle shape. Add every participant's headshot around the circle.

2. Share that Google Slides presentation with everyone, giving everyone edit access.

3. Ask team members to open that Google Slides presentation when the end of the gathering is near.

4. Designate one person who will start as the first storyteller. In the slide, the first storyteller draws a line from herself to the first recipient – this is a virtual yarn toss. Then the first storyteller shares a gratitude for learning from the first recipient.

5. The first recipient becomes the second storyteller and picks a second recipient, and the cycle continues.

6. A person can receive the yarn only once.

7. Repeat until everyone has held the yarn.

   Variation: Instead of using Google Slides, this ritual can be done in a digital whiteboard such as MURAL.

03 Virtual High-Quality Connection

Moment

People in the team or project work are new or indifferent to each other.

This is a **1:1 ritual**.

Intention

Connect people at a human level.

Time & Effort

The planning will be a quick 5–10 minutes if you assign people randomly. The ritual will take 10–15 minutes.

What is the ritual?

When we feel low energy from the people we meet, it drains our energy as well, especially in virtual meetings. Virtual High-Quality Connection is a simple ritual to charge virtual relationships. When the team lead is about to start a project she can ask the participants to form two-person duo teams; give them the prompt of "create a high-quality connection with your buddy"; give three further hints, shared goals, shared histories, and shared interests; set the time for 2 minutes for each person; and debrief when they come back from their connection rounds.

Backstory

High-quality connection is a term and exercise coined by Jane Dutton to energize workplace relationships with a positive attitude. According to Jane, high-quality connections are marked by mutual positive regard, trust, and active engagement on both sides. In a high-quality connection, people feel more open, competent, and alive (Dutton and Heaphy, 2016).

One central idea is that a high-quality connection doesn't need to take a long time to establish. These connections can happen in a short amount of time when two people find a commonality in a one-on-one interaction.

Jane adds: "Building good connective tissue at the beginning fundamentally alters the trajectory of possibilities for creativity, risk-taking, engagement, etc. Sometimes we forget the power of inviting people to use their ingenuity and power to build high-quality connections with others."

How it works

1. Inform people that they will be put into pairs.
   - You, the meeting organizer, decide whether you'd like pair assignments to be random or curated. (If curated, keep in mind that you will need to manually assign people into breakout rooms later.)
2. Describe the goal of the activity: "Your challenge is to form a high-quality connection with your partner."
3. Give instructions: "Each person will have 2 minutes to lead the connection building, Decide who in your pair will lead first. I'll let you know when two minutes is up and it's time to switch who leads."
4. Send pairs to virtual breakout rooms.
5. Give the first person 2 minutes to lead.
6. After 2 minutes, let everyone know that it's time to switch leads (e.g. broadcast a message to all breakout rooms).
7. Give the second person two minutes to lead.
8. After another two minutes, tell people to ask their partner what worked in building a high-quality connection. Give two minutes for this feedback conversation.
9. End the breakout rooms, and debrief together.

04 Smell Together

Moment

When people need a sense of togetherness for an opening moment.

This is a group ritual that can work for **small and large groups.**

Intention

Express gratitude for each other.

Time & Effort

Planning is relatively easy as it relies on the kitchen pantry. Actual ritual can take 5–7 minutes with intro and a debrief.

What is the ritual?

Have you ever found yourself missing the visceral feeling of enjoying your food at a social gathering, where the tastes, smells, and sounds made you feel part of a community?

Smell Together takes us through a sensory experience together as a group, even when people are in different places. Before a virtual meeting, the meeting organizer asks people to bring a certain spice, such as nutmeg or cinnamon. At the end of the meeting, the meeting organizer invites everyone to smell the spices that they brought. After the countdown, people smell the spices at the same time. This creates a co-sensory experience.

Backstory

The inspiration for this ritual came when we were listening to Priya Parker's podcast Together Apart (Parker, 2020). Priya got this question: How can people bring senses into virtual gatherings, when they are in different places? She was talking to 400 community members of Tri-faith – an internationally co-located group of congregations of Jewish, Christian, and Muslim faiths in Omaha. She then suggested to make it co-sensory by everyone bringing a spice to the side of their computers.

The question's reference point was the Jewish Havdalah, a ritual that marks the end of Shabbat and the beginning of the new week. In Havdalah, ritual participants smell sweet Havdalah spices (for example nutmeg or cinnamon) to mark that transition and center themselves before starting the new week. The smell's sensory experience brings the person to the moment, and "re-presence" their mind and body. This ritual also helps provide a mental and emotional grounding to the person to get ready for the upcoming week.

How it works

1. Pick a specific spice, such as cinnamon or nutmeg.

2. Ask people to bring the spice to the side of their computer before the meeting, for instance in your calendar invite.

3. At the beginning or ending of your meeting, invite people to the Smell Together.

4. Take three deep breaths to open up your sense of smell.

5. Now, invite everyone to smell the spice at the same time with a countdown.

6. Have a closure with people adding emoji or phrases on chat on what the smells evoke in them.

How to adapt

The gist of this ritual is to co-experience a sensory stimuli to have that feeling of co-presence. This means you can change the sensory stimuli based on the context. It can be touching the same prop, tasting the same food, listening to the same music. Another adaptation can be with food. People can actually sprinkle the spice on a pastry like a croissant.

05 Team Positivity Contagion

Moment

When people need to connect with their weak-tie relationships in a community.

This is a **large group ritual** that can be adjusted to small groups.

Intention

Create positive connection through virtual interactions.

Time & Effort

The setup will require some time and effort. The actual ritual will require the host to prepare the content.

What is the ritual?

Team Positivity Contagion is a collection of rituals that aim at keeping a community connected during the shelter-in-place at Stanford campus.

Community members can sign up to host and attend events by using communication tools such as Zoom, Google Calendar, and Slack. The events are self-vetted. The organizers set some basic principles such as openness, inclusivity, and positivity in virtual interactions. Hosts have created five types of events: physical well-being, socializing, cooking, skillsharing, and games. Sessions include Hot Pilates, Remote Dance Party, Sheer Relief Virtual Hair Cut, Sweet Potato Gnocchi, Everyday MakeUp Class, Virtual Spelling Bee. Hosts facilitated more than 140 events in a couple of months.

Backstory

This ritual series was created by a group of students from Stanford's Graduate School of Business during the COVID-19 shelter-in-place measures in California. When Christina Troitino realized that the shelter-in-place was not going away anytime soon, she first got panicked but then wondered if there could be a way to vitalize her relationships in her last semester before graduation. She also realized she can connect with her close-circle friends, but found it hard to connect with her weak-tie relationships. This led her to reach out to like-minded friends. Their conversations led them to come up with a program for a self-hosted event series that could generate positivity and rich virtual interactions.

The program's success led her to reach out to other graduate schools in the United States, such as University of Chicago Booth and Columbia. Her counterparts in those schools decided to adopt a similar program. Christina's team then created a playbook for schools that can create similar ritual programs within their communities. One highlight from the playbook is to create a Slack bot that can socialize the events across Slack channels.

How it works

1. Self elect to host a virtual event that would spark positivity.

2. Invite people to the event using Google Calendar and other channels.

3. Send a 15 minutes reminder before the event.

4. Run the event with a closure and send feedback forms afterward.

How to adapt

Christina and her friends at Stanford GSB created a playbook on how to adopt a similar ritual program at a school setting. The playbook gives suggestions on how to set a basic flow in calendar invitations, advertising, and creating a newsletter. They also have a couple of suggestions based on the learnings from 140 events. They learned that Zoom fatigue is real as people get closer to the end of the work week. They suggest creating events at the beginning of the week or during the weekends.

06 You Never Would Have Guessed

Moment
In one of the first few meetings of a new group.

This is a **small group ritual.**

Intention
See people as people and not just as job functions.

Time & Effort
Can be done in as little as 2 minutes.

What is the ritual?

This ritual helps meeting participants to see each other as human beings that exist beyond their job functions by surfacing surprises. We learn something new about each person that we never would have guessed.

This ritual is particularly useful in one of the first few meetings of a new group as people are getting to know each other, though it can also be used with more established groups who could use a nudge to treat each other more like human beings.

Backstory

Glenn created this ritual when co-teaching Design Across Borders at the Stanford d.school in Spring 2020, as a way to nudge students to get curious about each other's personal stories. He combined humanization and surprise.

Humanization translates into interpersonal treatment. Ashley Hardin, a former management consultant who is now a professor of organizational behavior, describes how knowledge we have about another person's life can humanize them and can change the way we treat them.

Surprise gets your attention and is more likely to be memorable. You might remember someone sharing "I like to jog," but you're much more likely to remember someone saying "I've defeated two world champions in judo."

How it works

1. This ritual can be done either at the beginning of a meeting as a warm-up, or it can be done in the middle of a meeting as a fun break between sections of a meeting.

2. The facilitator tells the group that we're going to do a short activity called "You Never Would Have Guessed."

3. The facilitator asks people to think of one thing about yourself that most people in this group would never have guessed about you, and gives everyone 10 seconds to think about it.

4. People then share that one thing. In smaller groups, people can share verbally. In larger groups, people can share in chat.

5. The facilitator closes the ritual by thanking everyone for sharing, and inviting everyone to ask others about what they shared at some point down the road.

GALLERY VIEW

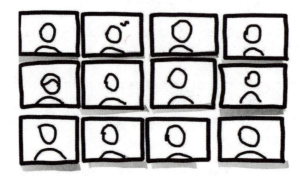

START WITH THE GALLERY
VIEW TO BETTER UNDERSTAND
THE GROUP, REACTIONS & MORE

SPEAKER VIEW

NOW SWITCH TO THE
SPEAKER VIEW, TILL YOU
GET TIRED. THEN GO TO ①

07 Conversation Cuts

Moment

When a group is trying to develop better virtual meeting habits.

This is a group ritual that can work for **small as well as large groups.**

Intention

Be more conscious of how we pay attention to each other.

Time & Effort

Takes 30 seconds to explain, and 5 seconds every so often to nudge people to try switching views.

What is the ritual?

Conversation Cuts is a ritual that can help people develop more effective habits of how they pay attention to different people in a virtual meeting.

In an in-person meeting, we are used to turning our head so that we can see the person speaking and then check how other people are reacting.

In a virtual meeting, we can develop new habits of how we direct our attention using what's available to us in a video call – switching back and forth between Speaker View and Gallery View.

In this ritual, the facilitator cues people with suggestions of when to switch to different views. These are suggestions only; participants are free to do what they feel most comfortable with.

Backstory

Glenn created this ritual when he noticed himself spacing out at a meeting where people were giving extended updates, talking for long stretches of time.

He first tried entire meetings in Speaker View in Zoom but didn't feel like he had a sense of the reactions of all the people in the room, and he was spacing out looking at one person for long stretches of time.

He then tried entire meetings in Gallery View, but then found he wasn't paying enough attention to the main speaker and that looking at everyone all the time induced a different kind of monotony that also caused him to space out.

Glenn thought back to his experience as the curator of TEDxPeacePlaza, which included being a part of the video production team. Specifically, Glenn thought about how he edited TEDx Talks that did not have slides, and how he'd cut between close-up shots, wide shots, and audience shots.

In his virtual meetings, Glenn experimented with flipping back and forth between Speaker View and Gallery View when a single person was speaking for long stretches of time, eventually settling into a rough ratio of two-thirds Speaker View and one-third Gallery View to read the room. With the varied views, and the active switching back and forth, Glenn found it easier to focus and stay engaged.

How it works

1. At the beginning of a section where a single speaker is going to talk for 5 minutes or more, the meeting facilitator invites participants to try the ritual while the speaker is speaking: "We're about to have some extended report outs. If you're feeling a little spacy or Zoomed out, or if you want to enhance your experience of this meeting, I invite you to try this practice called Conversation Cuts."

2. The facilitator explains the details: "The idea is simple – switch between Speaker View and Gallery View every so often. Use Speaker View to watch the active speaker, and use Gallery View to see how other are reacting.

3. The facilitator offers occasional reminders: "To help you remember to switch, I'll send occasional reminders to SWITCH in the chat. But those are just reminders to do some switching every so often. It is totally up to you when (and if) you switch.

08 Team Symbol

Moment
Early in a team's formation.

Intention
Create a shared identity with a visual symbol.

Time & Effort
We recommend allocating 30 minutes for this activity so you can get to a symbol your whole team can stand by. But it's possible that a team can coalesce around a symbol more quickly.

This is a **small group ritual** that can be adjusted to large groups.

What is the ritual?

Team Symbol is a ritual where a team chooses or creates a visual symbol of what they stand for together as a team. The symbol can embody the organization or team's vision, mission, and/or values.

The symbol could be a variety of things – a metaphor, a place, a historical reference, or other possibilities. And this does not have to be a fancy branding exercise. It can be as simple as pulling an image from the Internet or a simple hand sketch.

What's important is that it is a visual that reminds the team of what common purpose brings them and keeps them together.

Backstory

This ritual was inspired by the work of human rights activist Faisal Saeed Al Mutar, who founded Ideas Beyond Borders, a nonprofit that aims to empower the vulnerable with hope and prevent extremism before it takes root.

The Ideas Beyond Borders team has translated hundreds of pieces of literature and information – from best-selling books to articles and more – in the hopes of making inaccessible ideas accessible to Arabic speakers worldwide.

Faisal and his team wanted a symbol that inspired people and could tell the story of their vision without them having to explain it. They drew inspiration from the original Bayt Al Hikma, or House of Wisdom, a center for enlightened thought, pluralistic thinking, and scientific discovery that dominated the Golden Age of the Middle East. To represent their work, Ideas Beyond Borders uses the symbol of "House of Wisdom 2.0."

How it works

1. Early in a team's formation, schedule a 30-minute meeting to create a Team Symbol, a visual that will remind the team of what common purpose brings them and keeps them together.

2. At the beginning of the meeting, have the group brainstorm on this question: "What aspect of our vision, mission, or values do we want to constantly remind ourselves of?" Take 5 minutes for all team members to brainstorm in a shared online space, such as in Google Docs or MURAL.

3. Then take the ideas from Step 2, and group them into themes. Take 5 minutes to do this.

4. Then brainstorm possible visual symbols for the themes that emerged in Step 3. Take 10 minutes to brainstorm visual symbols.

5. Review the visual symbols that were brainstormed. Have the team decide, either through consensus or a vote, which symbol they would like to use.

Jane Dutton

Professor at Univ. of Michigan
(Emerita)

Jane Dutton is a professor of business administration and psychology at the University of Michigan. Her research lies at the intersection of strategy, management, organizations, and psychology. In her research, she focuses on how high-quality connections and identity processes increase employees' and organizations' capabilities.

The Emergence of High-Quality Connections

When Jane began teaching a course on professional relationships 20 years ago, she found very disconnected literature on how to create high-quality connections. This made her write a book on the topic to bring a holistic view of human connection. You will sense a high-quality connection when two people feel energized and have mutuality and positive regard for each other after the encounter. To create a high-quality connection, Jane Dutton discovered four pathways: respectfully engage others, task-enable others, trust others, and play.

These four paths are not independent of each other; they can happen at the same time. Whatever path someone is on, the first moments matter. She says "If you're thinking about complexity, theory, and theories of emergence the initializing conditions are really important. So what happens in the first three minutes or the first 40 seconds matters."

Over the years she learned that connecting with people is as important as the task itself. That's why she and her colleagues created an exercise that they run during workshops. (You can take a look at the Virtual High-Quality Connection Ritual in Chapter 7 which is inspired by their in-person exercise.)

Jane thinks when it comes to finding ways to connect "we're just limited by our imagination, we have to see investing in the quality of connection, as important as getting the task done. And that tilling the soil of connection, in terms of lifting up the potential for the capability of the collective, is an investment in the whole. It's an investment in the collective."

She gives the example of a personal letter she wrote to her students. During the COVID-19 pandemic, she had a seminar that she was going to teach virtually with 70 people over 3 hours. To create a high-quality connection, she decided to write a personal letter to all 70 of her students. She said part of the inspiration came from one of her former student's research. Ashley Hardin looked at four different work contexts and discovered that disclosing personal information about yourself humanizes the relationship between co-workers and increases interpersonal treatment. In her letter, Jane revealed more about her personal life than she used to do. But she thought this would make it easier for her students to connect to her, and it would provide more places for finding common ground. It also potentially made it more memorable and unique.

Creating high-quality connections for Jane is capacity building for employees and organizations as a whole. She emphasizes that "this is a source of human capacity building that does not cost money. It does not cost material resources. It just requires that we understand its power and how to unlock it." She also sees this capacity building as part of a repertoire building from which employees can pick different practices based on their needs.

She sees teaching people how to build high-quality connections as empowerment for people. She says, "This is about strength building for you to bear the weight of what the world's doing to you. So it's not just about good stuff. It's about being able to bear the weight of the bad stuff as well as putting you on a pathway."

As a closing thought, Jane thinks we all have a magic wand that we carry in our back pocket. We can always strengthen other people by how we interact with them. "We have the beautiful power to not only make someone stay, but to make someone breathe better, make someone's heart rate go down."

8

Rituals for

1:1 Meetings

When you want deeper conversations

When you have a meeting with only one other person, these rituals can help you connect to your partner and deepen the conversation. The rituals are good for encouraging the one-on-one partners to recognize each other's needs.

"There's something very real about helping someone one-on-one." – Matt Mullenweg

One-on-ones can be the epitome of personal attention and connection. Or they can fall disappointingly short of our expectations.

What if our virtual one-on-ones could help us deepen connections with each other, so that we could be more courageous, candid, and vulnerable with each other?

The rituals in Chapter 8 provide springboards for deepening connections. While many of these rituals could also be done in group settings with three or more people, we think they can be particularly strong in one-on-ones.

Special of the Week helps us understand what is most important to each other in the short term and why. **Battery Charger & Drainer** powers our sense of each other's energy. **Get Help / Give Help** clarifies mutual aid. **If Only ...** gets us to expand each other's sense of possibility. **Always Appreciate** is a different way to support each other's performance. **Life Stories** helps us understand how our pasts have shaped who we are today. **One Surprise** nudges us to find something new. **Uncommon Parallels** locates what uniquely ties us together.

8 Rituals for 1:1 Meetings

01 Special of the Week
What's Most Important This Week and Why?

02 Battery Charger & Drainer
What's Giving You Energy? What's Taking Away Energy?

03 Get Help / Give Help
Useful Help All Around

04 If Only...
The Impossible May Be More Possible

05 Always Appreciate
Gratitude Every Time We Meet

06 Life Stories
Something That Shaped Who You Are

07 One Surprise
Disrupt Clichéd Conversations

08 Uncommon Parallels
Similar in a Way That's Different

01 Special of the Week

Moment
During a regular check-in.

This is a **1:1 ritual**.

Intention
Better understand not only what someone is working on, but also what's most important and why.

Time & Effort
Takes 3 to 5 minutes.

What is the ritual?

Sometimes we think we understand what's important to someone, but it turns out we were totally misunderstanding. And sometimes, we have no idea what each other is doing!

Special of the Week helps us get into a regular rhythm of understanding not only what each of us is focused on, but also why. By understanding the why and the challenges involved, we can be more empathetic with and supportive of each other.

Understanding where each other is at, mentally and emotionally, is particularly important when we're interacting virtually.

Backstory

In a very indirect way, Special of the Week was inspired by produce. Not producing or productivity. Produce. Like fruits and vegetables produce.

The specials when you buy produce are often the things that are in season. Yes, you might be getting a great price on them, but more profoundly, you're getting them at their peak flavor.

If we can help each other cook up our freshest ingredients in our work, we might be able to create better-tasting results that pop.

How it works

1. During a regular 1:1 meeting, start the ritual by saying, "Let's talk about each other's Special of the Week." Explain that the Special of the Week is one thing at the top of your list for this week, one that is most urgent, important, or both.

2. One person asks the other person a series of questions:
   - "What's your Special of the Week? What are you most focused on doing and/or learning this week?"
   - "Why is that important?"
   - "What are the trickiest challenges involved?"
   - "Anything I can do to support you?"

3. Then trade places in terms of who is asking questions and who is answering them.

4. You might consider writing your Special of the Week in a shared Google Doc or MURAL canvas, and then comment and tag during the week when you have thoughts that percolate about each other's Specials.

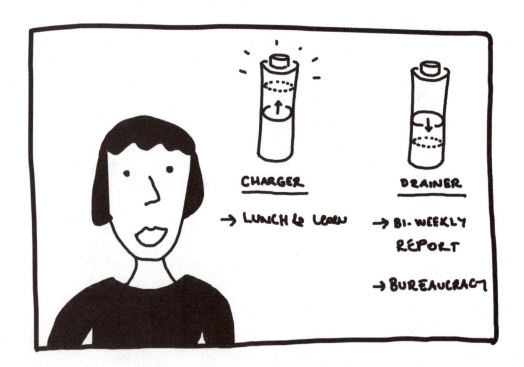

02 Battery Charger & Drainer

Moment
Can be one part of a regular one-on-one check-in.

This is a **1:1 ritual.**

Intention
Understand what's feeling motivating and what's feeling demotivating.

Time & Effort
The preparation will take silent reflection of 3–5 minutes. The ritual can be under 10 minutes.

What is the ritual?

Have you ever picked up your phone and were surprised that the battery was running low? "Wait, wasn't it 100% not that long ago?" And the you realize, "Oh wait, I've had YouTube running this whole time, playing videos for the last few hours! No wonder why my battery is gone … "

In this one-on-one ritual, we use the metaphor of your personal "battery" and you share with each other two things: 1) What is giving you energy (battery charger)? 2) What is draining your energy (battery drainer)?

As we understand each other's battery charge and drain, we might be able to offer more effective help and empathize with each other.

Backstory

Battery Charger & Drainer was inspired by Glenn's general paranoia of having his phone run out of battery. He constantly scans for power outlets in cafés, waiting areas, and airports. He occasionally wonders if he has left any one of three video recording apps accidentally running and draining battery.

How it works

1. Each person shares their battery charger and battery drainer.
   - A battery charger is something that is giving you energy, that is currently energizing you.
   - A battery drainer is something that is making you lose energy, that is currently dragging you down.

2. There are different ways you can share:
   - *Share verbally*. Simply describe your charger and drainer in words, out loud to each other – quick and easy.
   - *Write down, then share*. Each person takes a minute to write down some thoughts in a shared digital space. This gives people a chance to put together their thoughts, and also has the advantage of documenting it if that's helpful for remembering.
   - *Sketch and share*. Each person takes a minute or two to draw their battery charger and drainer. Make a simple sketch on paper. Then you show each other your sketches and quickly talk through them.

WHY? CAN YOU TELL ME MORE ABOUT THE CHALLENGE?

FOR X, I WAS WONDERING IF YOU COULD HELP ME BY ...

FOR Y, I COULD HELP YOU BY ....

FOR Z, THIS OTHER PERSON COULD HELP YOU BY ....

03 Get Help / Give Help

Moment
As part of a regular one-on-one check-in.

This is a **1:1 ritual.**

Intention
Understand specific ways you can help each other.

Time & Effort
Takes 3 to 5 minutes.

What is the ritual?

We often want to be helpful, particularly to our colleagues. But sometimes "let me know if I can helpful" isn't specific enough.

In Get Help / Give Help, we break it down just enough so that we can be more effective in helping each other.

Backstory

This ritual was designed by Glenn, inspired by the work of social psychologist Heidi Grant Halvorsen. Glenn was particularly interested in this passage from Heidi's book *Reinforcements: How to Get People to Help You*:

To provide assistance, your benefactor must notice your need and believe that you desire help. You can make this easier by making direct, explicit requests for help. Don't beat around the bush. He or she also needs to take responsibility for helping, which tends to happen more when requests are made to one individual specifically, rather than to a group at large. Last, your helper has a life, too. Make your request reasonable and clear, and be open to taking whatever help you can get. (Halvorsen, 2018)

How it works

1. Start with one person sharing one to three things they are working on and what's most challenging about each one.

2. The other person then asks clarifying questions. ("Why? Can you tell me more about ... ")

3. Then switch places, in terms of who's sharing and who's asking clarifying questions.

4. After both people have shared, get help and give help to each other.
    -   "For X, I was wondering if you could help me by ... "
    -   "For Y, I can help you by ... "
    -   "For Z, this other person might be able to help by ... "

IF ONLY ___
___
___

IS IT POSSIBLE
THAT COULD BE
TRUE, PERHAPS
UNDER CERTAIN..?

SAY MORE
WHY THAT
WOULD BE
HELPFUL ?

IF ONLY ___
___
___

04 If Only...

Moment
When you want a safe way to test the limits of what's possible.

This is a **1:1 ritual.**

Intention
Lightheartedly explore things that sound impossible or impractical.

Time & Effort
Takes 4–7 minutes.

What is the ritual?

Many times, there's more possible than we think, but we don't push the possibility frontier because of fear or because we think it's going to be a lot of work.

This ritual creates a regular occasion for us to lightheartedly explore the seemingly impossible with statements that start with "If only … " and follow-up questions about those statements.

It's understood that much of what we say in this ritual won't get anywhere, but we keep doing it to push ourselves in a fun way, and we might eventually find some unexpected possibilities. And it might just make us smile and laugh. :)

Backstory

The If Only ... ritual was inspired by John Bielenberg and his Think Wrong ways. John believes that thinking wrong – thinking impossible, ridiculous, or the-worst-thing-we-could-do thoughts – can be a powerful way to disrupt the heuristic pathways in our brains in order to find new possibilities.

How it works

1. Each person shares one "If only ... " statement. We encourage each other to make statements that may sound impossible or ridiculous. Start the statement "If only ... " and complete it with something that could make your work better in some way. Examples:
    *   "If only 1 p.m. Pacific could be everyone's mandatory nap time."
    *   "If only we could use our training budget for VR goggles."
    *   "If only upper management were all fanatic fans of *The Simpsons*."

2. After each person shares, ask each other nudging questions:
    *   "Say more about why that would be helpful?"
    *   "Is it possible that could be true, perhaps under certain circumstances?"
    *   "That may never happen, but what if this [more plausible] thing were to happen?"

3. See if there's anything that might be actionable that comes out of the conversation. And don't worry if there's not. Sometimes it's just a passing thought. Sometimes it needs time to marinate and lead to future ideas.

4. Thank each other for your If Only ... statements.

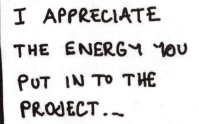

05 Always Appreciate

Moment
End of a one-on-one check-in.

This is a **1:1 ritual**.

Intention
Regularly express appreciation for each other's efforts.

Time & Effort
Super easy – takes 2 minutes. It doesn't take much time to thank someone. :)

What is the ritual?

How often have you heard someone say, "You know, people express their appreciation of my work waaaay too much. I'm soooo tired of people thanking me all the time!" This happens ... never. (Okay, maybe there are a few people who are so fortunate.)

Most of us don't get thanked enough for the work we do. This ritual helps us to get into a regular habit of expressing appreciation and receiving appreciation for each other's specific efforts.

Backstory

This ritual was inspired by a story that Odmaa Byambasuren told Glenn about a ritual that she practices. Odmaa shared what it was like to write down something she was grateful for 21 days in a row. That high frequency of gratitude expression changed her mindset. She found out just how many different things she was grateful for, things that she had not previously noticed or considered.

Later, Glenn wondered, what if that kind of practice was applied to our interactions with people we talk with on a regular basis?

How it works

1. This ritual works best with people who you meet with one-on-one on at least a semi-regular basis.

2. Each time you meet, at the beginning or end of your meeting, each of you expresses one appreciation of the other person.

    Try to be specific if you can be. But the most important thing is to express some kind of gratitude.

    Here are some sample starter statements:
    *   "I appreciate what you did with … "
    *   "I appreciate how you … "
    *   "I appreciate the thought … "
    *   "I appreciate your dedication to … "
    *   "I appreciate your energy around … "

06 Life Stories

Moment

In one of your initial meetings as you get to know someone.

This is a **1:1 ritual**.

Intention

Understand one thing from a person's life history that has influenced who they are today.

Time & Effort

This takes about 10 minutes to do. It's possible to do more quickly, though it's the kind of thing you don't want to rush.

What is the ritual?

Sometimes it helps to understand a bit about where each other is coming from in a bigger picture sense. What are some of the more important reasons why you are who you are today?

Life Stories is a ritual about getting to know each other more as people by asking for one story: What's one thing that has shaped who you are today?

Backstory

Life Stories is based on a hypothesis: When people tell us about an experience that has shaped who they are today, it can not only help us develop more empathy for them, but can also help build a connection. Sharing such a story is a way in which we make ourselves vulnerable and seen. And it's also probably going to be a story that you're going to remember!

How it works

1. Think about one experience that has shaped who you are today. It doesn't have to be the most important or the most influential experience. It can be anything that has had an effect that has stayed with you. Let's take 1 minute to think about that and silently put together some thoughts.

2. Take 4 minutes each to tell each other a life story.

3. After your partner has shared their story, thank her or him for sharing.

    Optional: Ask each other one follow-up question about your respective stories.

07 One Surprise

Moment
At a regular one-on-one check-in.

This is a **1:1 ritual.**

Intention
Share something unexpected that has happened since last time we met.

Time & Effort
Takes 2–5 minutes.

What is the ritual?

Sometimes we go into autopilot when catching up.

"How are you?"
"Fine. Busy. And you?"
"Fine. Busy too."
"Yeah."
"Yeah."

This ritual prompts us to share the unusual or surprising, which can often lead to more curiosity questions, and sometimes to new opportunities.

Backstory

Asking people about things that surprised them helps nudge them out of autopilot and consider something that could change the way they see the world. Surprises can also signal to our brain, "Hey, you might want to pay extra attention here, because this here isn't something you already know." One Surprise combines these nudges of surprises with nudges toward curiosity and interest.

How it works

1. Ask each other: "What's one surprising thing that happened to you this week?"

2. After each person shares their surprising thing, express interest and curiosity with statements and questions such as:
    - "Whoa, that is crazy!"
    - "Can you say more about why that was surprising to you?"
    - "What do you make of it?"

08 Uncommon Parallels

Moment

In an early meeting where we are getting to know each other.

This is a **1:1 ritual.**

Intention

Find one thing we have in common that most people don't have in common.

Time & Effort

Takes 4–7 minutes to do.

What is the ritual?

One way in which we can more strongly relate to a person is to find a similarity that makes us different from most others.

In Uncommon Parallels, you find one thing that the two of you have in common that most people in your team, organization, etc. don't have in common.

And if you're ambitious, you can extend to finding three different things you have in common that most people don't.

Backstory

Glenn developed Uncommon Parallels by applying one approach in design synthesis to human connection.

In design synthesis, we derive insights as we look across all of the information and data we have collected. One way to work our way toward insights is to look for distinct similarities. For example, "How are these five things alike in a way that no other things are alike? And what's behind that distinct similarity?"

Using this approach, perhaps we can find deeper human connections by finding our distinct similarities and what lies behind them.

How it works

1. Begin the ritual with this point of departure: "Let's figure out one thing that you and I have in common, that is different than most other people in our team/organization."

2. Take 3 minutes to brainstorm many different possibilities of what you might have in common.

3. Evaluate each possibility.
    - Is it a real and accurate similarity?
    - Are there many other people in our team/organization who are similar to us in that way, or is it just the two of us?

4. Keep going until you find at least one uncommon parallel. If you're ambitious, you can aim to find three uncommon parallels.

Jesper Frøkjær Sørensen

Associate Professor, Department of the Study of Religion, Aarhus University

Work on Rituals

Professor Jesper Sørensen works at the intersection of cognitive, cultural, and social systems. His work on rituals looks at how people process "ritual" behavior in comparison to more ordinary behavior.

In one such study, Jesper and his colleague Kristoffer Nielbo found that when people are experiencing a ritual, they are less able to predict what is going to happen or coast on "autopilot." There is no predictable cause-and-effect sequence of actions, so people must use a significant part of their cognitive energy to process the ritual sequences. The ritual swamps their working memory.

According to Jesper, rituals require people to pay more attention to what is happening – and this attentiveness has important side effects. First of all, your working memory is consumed by fully paying attention to the moment. Second, you start making secondary interpretations of symbolic elements in the ritual. You begin associating specialness to the objects and phrases. Third, your emotions are all-in, which aligns your emotions with others', creating social cohesion while syncing with other people.

Jesper has also studied how meaning-making works in ritual. We create meaning in three phases: pre-ritual, during-ritual, and post-ritual. As counterintuitive as it may seem, we don't make most of the meaning during the ritual itself, since we are so consumed by paying attention to the ritual. Most of the meaning really arrives after the actions. After the ritual, we reconstruct the events to make sense of what happened. We create a story that elevates our ordinary experience into a special one.

Rituals as Cultural Technologies

Jesper sees rituals as cultural technologies that simultaneously produce different effects on people. That might be why they are so successful. He gives the example of a Catholic Eucharist ritual. Some people would participate in this ritual, and they would think deeply afterward about its semantic meaning, and how this relates to the larger universe. Some others are there for the community. They'd say, "Hey, it was so nice to be in the congregation with so many other people." Others would say, "I went to the Eucharist and when I took the bread, I really thought about my sick mother and I hoped that this would direct energy toward her fighting disease," or "I have a heart condition that I really hope touching this would somehow help me fight." All these things can work together at the same time. That's the beauty of the ritual.

Jesper finds the distinction between ritual and ritualized action important. In a relatively long gathering like a wedding, you alternate between the ordinary and ritualized actions. If you ritualize every step of a wedding, it would be too difficult for people to participate in it. In a way, you need to give mental and emotional space for people to make sense of the ritual and reconstruct its meaning.

Recommendation to Others

In the context of workplace rituals, he suggests looking at what people are already doing and building on their ritualized behaviors. He emphasizes that people create ritualized behaviors spontaneously to form groups. He gives the example of youth rituals where teenagers bond by forming rituals like secret handshakes.

He suggests bringing the aesthetic aspects of rituals to the fore. Make rituals beautiful experiences so people will engage with it. Sometimes if you are too explicit about your intentions, people might feel they are being manipulated and will be more likely to react negatively. When reflecting on the tech companies that have teams across countries, he points to the importance of cultural context. If a company has offices in Bangalore and Palo Alto, the employees may have very different cultural references and contexts, which are likely to shape very different rituals. What you can do on Fridays before the weekend in Palo Alto and Bangalore is quite different.

Jesper also points to the differences between how people talk about activities that are rituals but that they don't necessarily call rituals. He suggests tuning into how people in your community are talking about rituals or common behavior, without necessarily using the word *ritual* when you ask. For example, you can ask people "So describe to me, what do you do when you meet?"

Sometimes you might be trying to establish a new ritual in your team, but the word *ritual* might have baggage for people in your context. If that's the case, simply don't refer to it as a ritual.

Rituals can also be a part of a larger strategy, especially for two key aspects of organizational culture. First, rituals can help establish and keep alive the organization's history and identity. Rituals can help companies reinforce their identity by reenacting their history and the behaviors of their key figures. Second, rituals can also help companies to reinforce innovation and creativity – defining their future work and evolution of their culture.

9

Rituals for Transitions and Shifting Culture

These rituals provide a safe space for individuals and teams to embrace change. They can let people reframe their intentions, and build energy for upcoming work.

"It is when we are in transition that we are most completely alive."
– William Bridges

Have you ever found yourself needing more mental and emotional space when transitioning between your family and home life? Or when moving from one meeting to the next? Or when moving into a new role that required a new mindset?

Transitions put a load on our adaptation muscles. Rituals can help with transitions. Rituals create space to anticipate what's next and release what's done.

The rituals in Chapter 9 address transitions at different scales including daily transitions, role transitions, and mindset transitions.

The Day Finale and **The Fake Commute** create boundaries and anchor moments to improve the daily transitions between home to work. **New Hire Intro** welcomes a new employee with warmth and humor. **The Festschrift Farewell** sends a departing employee off in a caring and appreciative way.

The other four rituals are more about transitioning into new mindsets to shift culture. **How We Roll** transitions a project team to a collaborative mindset. **Hero's Check-In** reimagines the employee's role in a performance review. **Meet n' Three** infuses a collaborative mindset across different tenures and disciplines. The **Unlearn Moment** shifts people from a fixed mindset to a growth mindset.

8 Rituals for Transitions and Shifting Culture

01 New Hire Intro
Onboarding Employees Like Leaders

02 The Day Finale
Marking the Boundary Between Work and Other Roles

03 The Festschrift Farewell
Farewelling a Leaving Employee

04 Meet n' Three
Shifting Culture One Lunch at a Time

05 How We Roll
Kicking Off Projects with a Collaborative Mindset

06 Hero's Check-In
Acknowledging the Modes of Career Growth

07 The Fake Commute
Marking the Transition with Physical Cues

08 The Unlearn Moment
Shifting Culture by Unlearning Old Habits

01 New Hire Intro

Moment

When a new employee joins virtually.

This is a **large group ritual** that can be adjusted to a small group.

Intention

Jump-start human connection from the get-go.

Time & Effort

Preparation will take less time. Give 5–7 minutes for the onboarding depending on the number of people.

What is the ritual?

The New Hire Intro is a ritual that a new employee goes through when they get onboarded to a company. Like a leader, they take the stage in an all hands meeting, and respond to three questions that are asked by the all hands host. These three questions help the rest of the team better understand and relate to the new team member. It also helps the new team member bond faster as he/she shares something personal about themselves from the beginning. This culture sets up the tone that it's okay to share things that are more personal and weird around your coworkers.

Backstory

This ritual came from MURAL, the hybrid remote company that created the leading digital workspace for visual collaboration. Mark Tippin leads the Learning Experience team and shared this ritual with us. He mentioned this ritual originated from Mariano Suarez-Battan, MURAL's CEO. When Mark went through the process himself, he shared that he used to have a mohawk and played in a punk rock group. This idea of sharing your weirdness opens people up to be vulnerable. That vulnerability builds trust. It breaks down the barriers and gives people something to talk about beyond their job titles.

How it works

1. When a new employee joins, introduce them as part of an all hands meeting.

2. Ask them the following questions:
    - "Why did you join this company? Why this company over any of the other options you have?"
    - "What's the impact you're looking forward to making here? Now that you're here, what's your purpose? What do you hope to achieve?"
    - "Tell us something really weird about you that no one else knows."

3. While they are answering these questions, those listening share their reactions with emoji and memes to other channels.

4. When they answer the last question, celebrate their response and welcome them one more time to the group.

02 The Day Finale

Moment

When it's time to transition back
to home and social life.

This is a **personal ritual.**

Intention

Mentally switch modes from work
to home.

Time & Effort

It will take 1–3 minutes depending
on the length of the reflection.

What is the ritual?

The Day Finale is a simple ritual where an individual employee declares that
the work is not finished but it's done at the moment, and it is time to focus on
other aspects of life outside work.

This is a personal ritual, but it can also be adapted for teams, as a closure to
their day. The team lead invites teammates to share with each other what
they are looking forward to after the day is over.

Backstory

When people work from home, there's a real need to make a clear and clean transition from work to home and vice versa. In the physical world, we do this by commuting from work to home. In virtual, this is not that easy. People can be connected 24/7. To overcome this, one can make the role transition an explicit intention setting. The idea to recognize that we have multiple roles outside of work comes from Shawn Johal. We can be parents, partners, competitive athletes, aspiring artists. To recognize this explicitly could make the transition easier and amplify the roles outside work (Goff-Dupont, 2020).

How it works

1. Set a daily reminder for your Day Finale on your phone.

2. When the reminder pings you, it's time to close all the work channels, pause notifications.

3. Acknowledge the moment, and close your laptop.

4. Declare that: "Now that my workday is done. I am freed up to be the best _____ (role: dad, wife, athlete) I can be."

5. Tonight after work, I want to make sure that _____ (what you want to accomplish today).

6. This intention setting will help you visualize and reinforce your holistic self, beyond work.

You can adapt the Day Finale to a team meeting. Pick a meeting that makes sense to have a Day Finale. Pose this question, what would you want to accomplish today after work today? Give 1–2 minutes for each team member to declare their intention.

03 The Festschrift Farewell

Moment
When an employee is leaving the company or retiring.

This is a **small group ritual** that can be adjusted to a large group.

Intention
Recognize and honor the person leaving the company.

Time & Effort
The planning will require a prep meeting and personal preparation for stories. Actual session can be 30–60 minutes.

What is the ritual?

Festschrift is a farewell meeting for a departing teammate, where team members share their memories. This happens when the teammate is still on the team, perhaps in their last week. The departing teammate also shares memories with the team.

Festschrift is a term borrowed from German, and means "celebration writing" (literally: feast-script). In academia, Festschrift is a book honoring a respected person during their lifetime.

Backstory

We came across this ritual through Mike Howley. Before his passing away, his friends at MIT put together a virtual Festschrift (Evers, 2020). The host of the ritual was Peter Sagal from NPR's "Wait, Wait, Don't Tell Me." The ritual's highlight was when Mike shared his thoughts and feelings. Celebrating your teammate when they are still on the team shows deeper values like care, joy, and loyalty. It also signals to the rest of the team that they matter even when they decide to leave the team.

How it works

1. When an employee announces that they are leaving the company, have an open call for people to be the Festschrift host.

2. Then invite people to think about a couple of stories that they found meaningful in their interactions with their departing colleague.

3. As the Festschrift meeting begins, host opens up the floor thanking the person leaving.

4. For 3–5 minutes, people share stories and memories.

5. Close the Festschrift by giving the departing colleague a chance to share their own stories.

6. Close the Festschrift virtually toasting drinks together.

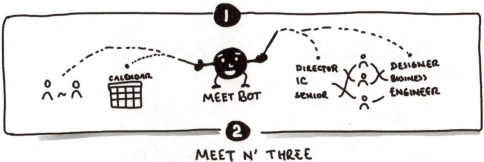

MEET N' THREE

REPEAT W NEW PEOPLE

04 Meet n' Three

Moment

When the team wants creative collisions across functions/departments.

This is **a small group ritual.**

Intention

Increase serendipity and connection from different roles, tenure.

Time & Effort

High effort to create the benefit and an automated bot. Once the setup is made, easier to arrange the date.

What is the ritual?

Meet 'n Three is an informal lunch date between three employees from different functions and tenure in the same organization. It's intentionally three people to lower the barrier of awkwardness of 1:1 lunches.

Meet 'n Three aims to bring serendipity and creative collisions by mixing and matching people based on role (data scientist, designer, financial analyst), and tenure (director, individual contributor, a manager). You can do this matching manually, or with the help of a smart bot.

Backstory

This ritual is from IDEO Chicago. In 2018, a team made up of workplace experience director Annette Ferrara, data scientists Jane Zanzig and Lisa Nash, and leadership coordinator Biz Wells worked on a bot called Meaty the Meet Bot. (On dictionary.com, a bot is a software program that can execute commands, reply to messages, or perform routine tasks, as online searches, either automatically or with minimal human intervention.) They were aware of bots like Donut for Slack that arrange 1:1 coffee dates, but wanted to lessen the awkwardness of 1:1 meetings, increase serendipitous interactions, and help new colleagues in a rapidly growing studio get to know each other more quickly. To make the benefit more enticing, individuals who go on a Meet n' Three get a stipend to pay for their lunches.

With the help of data scientists, the team automated the matching process with a bot powered by an algorithm. They trained the algorithm to maximize diversity of tenure and roles when selecting three people and used Google Calendar's open API to automatically arrange a lunch date on people's calendars. The Meet n' Three benefit adjusted well to the virtual context and they even expanded it to include colleagues in their Cambridge and New York studios.

How it works

1. Meaty the Meet Bot scrapes an internal company database for information like length of employment, discipline, career level, whether people have worked on projects together before, etc., to form triads or groupings of three people that might not otherwise cross paths in their day-to-day activities. These triads are assigned a novelty score.

2. The algorithm optimizes the score for an entire month's worth of groups using a Monte Carlo approach. (In other words, Meaty creates many more groups than are needed, and throws away all but those with the highest scores.)

3. Next, Meaty scrapes the triad's Google Calendars to find a lunch date that month that will likely work for the group.

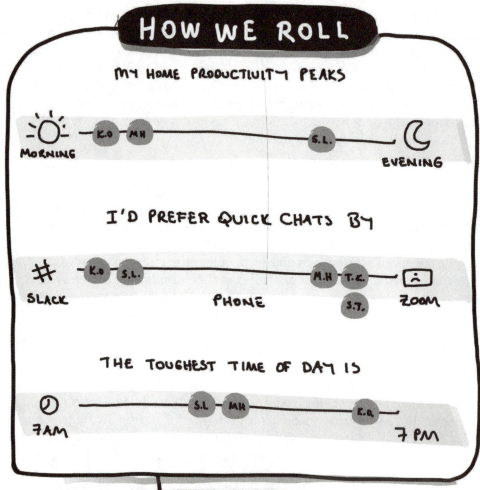

05 How We Roll

Moment
When a new project kicks off.

This is a **small group ritual.** It can be adjusted to bigger groups.

Intention
Foster empathy and understanding to increase collaboration between team members.

Time & Effort
Low effort since the templates are self-explanatory. Reviewing and having a consensus on preferences might take time.

What is the ritual?

How We Roll is a project kick-off ritual for team members to share their personal working styles and preferences in order to create a collaboration model as a team.

How We Roll helps each individual express the conditions that bring out their best. This is especially important in times where people have to juggle between home, work, and family responsibilities, such as during the COVID-19 pandemic of 2020.

This ritual is one of the first things a new team can do together when a project begins. It helps team members quickly learn each other's working styles and preferences, build rapport, and increase trust.

Backstory

How We Roll comes from the transformation consultancy SYPartners. It began as an in-person ritual and was quickly adapted to virtual when the COVID-19 pandemic forced people to work from home.
When a group of people is coming together for the first time, How We Roll fosters greater understanding and respect for one another as colleagues and teammates. The ritual helps create a strong interpersonal foundation to do great work together.

How it works

1. On a shared editable online tool such as Google Slides, create a selection of spectrums that speak to working preferences.

    Some spectrums might be:
    *   Early Bird <--> Night Owl.
    *   My home productivity peaks ... (in the morning <--> in the evening).
    *   I'd rather have ... (more heads down time <--> more team working).
    *   I'd prefer quick chats by ... (Slack <--> Phone <--> Zoom).
    *   The toughest time of the day is ... (7 a.m. <--> 2 p.m. <--> 10 p.m).
    *   I'd rather show work ... (in the morning <--> in the afternoon).
    *   My energy is boosted by ... (team process <--> team fun).

2. Each team member denotes their preferred way of working by adding their initials along each spectrum.
    *   Ask team members to create a circle shape and then double click on it to add their initials.

3. After each member has entered their preferences on the Google Slide, the team reviews the results together and plans their ways of working accordingly (e.g. no meetings before 10 a.m.; Slack questions instead of emailing; only one video meeting a day).

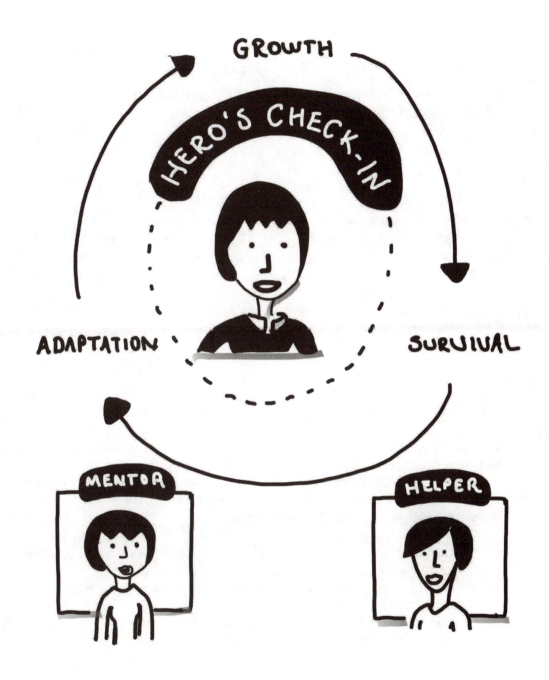

06 Hero's Check-In

Moment
When managers and employees want to have a performance review conversation.

This is **a 1:1 ritual.**

Intention
Foster understanding and empathy.

Time & Effort
The pre-ritual takes time to reflect. The actual ritual can be part of 30- to 60-minute conversations.

What is the ritual?

Hero's Check-In is a ritual to facilitate honest and positive conversations between employees and their managers. Often, performance reviews focus on assessment, with the experience led by the managers. This ritual reimagines the individual employee as the "Hero" of their story, supported by their manager ("Mentor") and colleagues ("Helpers").

Rather than assessment, the conversation is focused on support and enablement. Acknowledging that work is but one small part of our lives, the employee is asked to reflect and identify what mode they are in:
Survival: feeling they're just trying to stay above water
Adaptation: making adjustments to respond to challenges
Growth: taking the next step in their career journey

Backstory

This ritual is inspired by a mid-year review process used at the transformation consultancy SYPartners, developed by Bree Groff, Susan Burrows, and Peggie Sweeney. This ritual also draws inspiration from Joseph Campbell's Hero's Journey.

When the entire company shifted to virtual work in the wake of COVID-19, SYPartners redesigned their mid-year review process to better meet the needs of its employees. They recognized stress levels and emotions varied from person to person, and that this affected how people showed up at work. At one end, some individuals were struggling to get through the workday, and at the other, some were itching with a desire for new challenges.

To meet people where they were, the new review process evoked the metaphor of the Choose Your Adventure book series, in which the reader is able to choose and create their own reading experience. Similarly, in Hero's Check-In, the employee chooses their review "adventure" – personalizing it for their current needs.

How it works

1. The Hero sets up a 30-min conversation with their Mentor, and a few weeks later, a second 50-min meeting.

2. During this initial meeting, the Hero identifies to their Mentor what mode(s) they're in given how they're feeling with all that's going on in the world. (In 2020, examples included COVID-19, racial injustice, the climate crisis, and all stress related to these issues and others.) Together, they make a plan for feedback, such as who they should ask for feedback and what to focus on in their second feedback conversation.

3. The Hero then asks two to five colleagues to be Helpers on their career journey, and sets up a time to have a feedback conversation with them.

4. The Hero asks the Helpers three to five questions to discuss based on the mode(s) they're in. (E.g. If the Hero is 100% survival mode, this means three to five questions from the survival question bank.)

5. After these conversations, the Hero reflects on what they heard.

6. In the second meeting, the Hero and their Mentor unpack what came up in their feedback conversations with Helpers. Through their conversation, the Hero and their Mentor reach a mutual understanding about what the Hero needs to feel supported in their work and enabled to grow as they choose.

07 The Fake Commute

Moment
At the beginning of your workday.

This is a **personal ritual.**

Intention
Transition to work mode.

Time & Effort
10–15 minutes. Can be extended if desired.

What is the ritual?

As its name suggests, the Fake Commute is leaving the house to take a walk or to ride your bike around the block to mark the transition from home to work.

When you work from home, it helps to create a physical and mental boundary between different roles and modes. You can make it complete by taking a shower and dressing up for the office to prime yourself with a work mindset.

Backstory

Kursat created this ritual with his family for his own workdays. The first days of work from home were relatively novel, and his energy level starting the day was fine. However, over time he felt the drain and monotony when both home and work were in one place.

That's how the Fake Commute started. He and his family took walks around the block after breakfast to signal to both the parents and the kids that this is a transition to work time. When they came back, Kursat started his work-day in his garage. Kursat crossed the home to work boundary as he entered the garage.

How it works

1. Find an anchor moment for your fake commute. For instance, your anchor could be when you finish your cereal or coffee.

2. Once the moment kicks in, get ready for your commute. You can take a shower and change clothes.

3. If you live with someone, say, "Bye, will be back soon."

4. Take a good 10–15 minute walk. Experiment to find a route that gives you that length of time.

5. Once you come back home, find your anchor object for work. It can be your notebook, laptop, or your desk.

6. If you have the flexibility, assign a space for your work, so you can leave the office space at the end of the day, take your back-to-home commute, and start your evening.

MAKING SNAP JUDGMENTS WHEN AN IDEA IS PRESENTED FIRST TIME.

INTRODUCING MYSELF THE SAME WAY EVERY TIME VS. CREATIVE INTROS.

BEING SERIOUS ALL THE TIME.

MAKING MY CASE EXCLUSIVELY WITH POWER POINT.

WHAT'S ONE THING THAT YOU WANT TO UNLEARN THIS YEAR?

UNINTENTIONALLY INTERRUPTING PEOPLE BEFORE THEY'VE FINISHED TALKING.

OVER-DOMINATING CONVERSATIONS DURING GROUP MEETINGS.

FORGETTING APPRECIATING TEAMMATES FOR THEIR WORK.

WAITING FOR MY MANAGER TO NUDGE ME TO EXPRESS MY OPINION.

08 The Unlearn Moment

Moment

When there's a need to reflect and shift mindsets.

This is a **small group ritual.**

Intention

Shift from fixed mindset to growth mindset.

Time & Effort

10–15 minutes depending on the size of the group. You can timebox it.

What is the ritual?

The Unlearn Moment is a ritual for teams to reflect on existing mindsets, beliefs, and behaviors that they need to let go of, to open up space for more healthy habits. Sometimes the inhibitors for healthy habit formation are people's existing behaviors and mindsets. The prerequisite to behavior change is to unlearn some existing behaviors and mindsets. This simple ritual can be used in workshop settings as well as regular team meetings.

Backstory

This ritual comes from Shahid Khan, a senior business designer at SAP Labs, who works on digital transformation projects with C-level executives. He uses the Unlearn Moment ritual during the beginning of design thinking engagements, to nudge participants to reflect on their mindsets. Shahid thinks this ritual helps people question their existing mindsets. The question asked is a simple one, but can make people easily uncomfortable because it requires vulnerability.

Shahid finds the ritual an eye-opener for some people. It helps them to shift from a fixed mindset to a growth mindset. This distinction of mindsets was developed by Carol Dweck (Dweck, 2007).

The Unlearn Moment can also open up a group for more honest conversations. For instance, in one of Shahid's workshops, the CEO said, "I need to unlearn killing projects too soon." This honest reflection created a psychologically safe space for the rest of the two days. At the end of second day, the CEO said he didn't know his employees were this creative.

How it works

1. At the beginning of a workshop style meeting where you want to change the team's mindset (e.g. they believe that they can't be creative), ask them:

    - "What's one thing you want to unlearn this year?"
    - "Why do you want to unlearn that thing?"

2. Give them 2 minutes to write them down.

3. Ask the first person to come forward and share their unlearn moment.

4. Then the person shares with the rest "what they want to unlearn and why." Repeat with the entire group one by one.

5. Debrief at the end based on similarities and nuances.

Joumana Mattar

Service & Organizational Change
Manager at 4AM | An EY Venture

Work on Rituals

Joumana Mattar is a service designer
and a certified coach who creates
and facilitates processes for people
in order to effectively change organizations. Her journey with rituals
began when she founded her consultancy Madrid, owning the end-to-end
engagements with clients. Orches-
trating the entire process gave her
freedom to prototype and incorpo-
rate different experiences, such as
rituals. For instance, she discovered
that opening and closing rituals
are critical to creating engagement
when working with people who have
never experienced design thinking
before. Rituals are useful to connect
people with each other at the human
level, beyond their titles, to integrate
the meeting learnings, personal
takeaways, and have closure with
commitments at the end. Over the
years, her confidence in rituals grew
as she witnessed how they empow-
ered teams, and she tested them

beyond the design community and
in more corporate settings and with
C-suite stakeholders.

Learnings and Impact

Joumana believes rituals become
powerful when you can clearly articulate their purpose and intention.
This intentionality aspect differen-
tiates ritual from a less thought-out
warmup. Rituals help teams to
manage team dynamics such as
channeling disruptive energy and de-
mocratizing participation. Rituals can
also bring more impact to meetings
as they help people to visualize and
make their thoughts and feelings tangible. Visualizing creates a common
understanding and aligns people.

Joumana frames rituals as a dance or
a musical performance. The experience should include rhythm and
variety. Rhythm brings in familiarity,
whereas variety brings novelty. As a

designer, she needs to find a sweet spot between both and is constantly challenging herself to create rituals that fit the client and context. With rhythm and repetition, she creates a structure where people feel safe and share freely. By using a variety of techniques, she invites people to engage all their senses (sound, smell, touch, sight) to experience something unique, energizing, and memorable.

She knows that a ritual has stuck when she hears from clients that they applied it with their teams and tweaked it to fit their context. Hearing about adaptation stories is one of her proud moments as a coach. For instance, one of her customers from Portugal adapted Joumana's Talking Stick ritual and picked a light saber as their talking stick, which reflected that team's Star Wars loyalty. She also knows a ritual has stuck when it creates an expectation among teams – people ask for it when you skip it, considering it important enough to include in the agenda.

Recommendations to Others

Joumana emphasizes that you have to believe in the ritual yourself and embody it as a role model. This will help you create buy-in from participants and be perceived as authentic. She picks rituals that she can stand behind. Sometimes she doesn't call it a ritual since the word *ritual* is too loaded for a particular context and can be counterproductive to the final result.

Her other suggestion is to think of rituals as a dynamic process – as opposed to a rigid structure – which grows over time. To keep a ritual fresh, she suggests looking for inspiration in unexpected places (theater, arts, streets) and sustaining a sense of wonder in shaping them. You need to integrate more channels for communication in order to offer new ways for people to respond to the meeting topics as opposed to just reacting to them. For instance, she uses chat and polling to increase ways to interact as opposed to only video and verbal feedback. She finds props like a gong useful to invite people to participate in a fun and unexpected way.

Finally, she suggests practicing to get better at rituals. The more you practice rituals, the more you get to a sense of flow where you embody the script and adapt to real-time feedback, instead of just following it to the letter, regardless of impact.

Expectations for the Future

Joumana thinks working virtually has surfaced a new kind of vulnerability, a digital vulnerability. When we open our camera, we share our personal space. When we start adding content in real-time on tools like Google Slides, or Miro, we leave little room for processing our thoughts. She finds recognizing this vulnerability as a first step to move forward. In the future, people will find healthier boundaries and transitory spaces to work with this vulnerability.

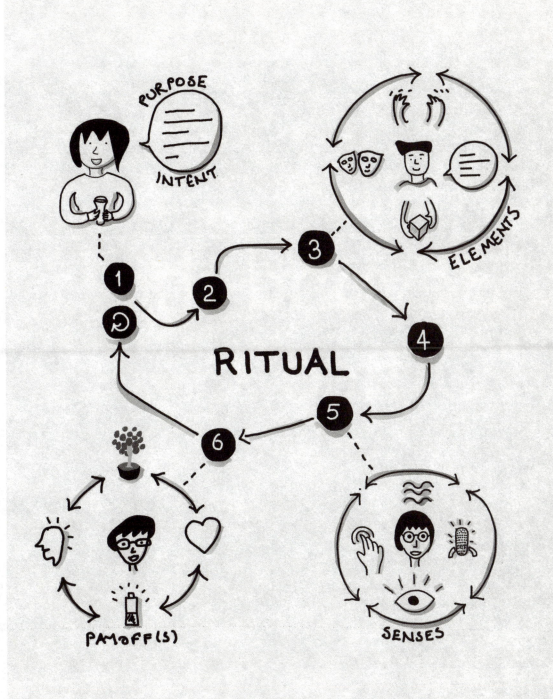

PART THREE

Beyond the "Office"

10
Rituals for Teaching and Training Online

This section is specifically for teachers and students, to improve online class meetings. These rituals can help them see each other's human side, and to energize them together to create an active learning environment.

"I entered the classroom with the conviction that it was crucial for me and every other student to be an active participant, not a passive consumer ... education as the practice of freedom ... education that connects the will to know with the will to become.
– bell hooks

As design educators ourselves, we are optimistic about what's possible with teaching and training online, but we are also ruggedly realistic about where we are today. Teachers in 2020 heroically did their best when the world was turned upside down almost overnight, but there's still much to figure out.

The rituals in Chapter 10 offer starting points that focus on the human side of virtual learning, helping students become active learners. **Hand Shake Down** energizes and synchronizes a class from the get-go. **Pass the Question** nudges a class to revolve around the students instead of the instructor. **Two Point Mashup** encourages students to synthesize and build on each other's thoughts. **Hand Signal Expressions** enable students to express themselves while keeping the flow of the class. **Pass the Mic** helps students to be heard as well as focus their listening. **Previous Episode** connects the longer arc of a course across class sessions. **Opening Credits** makes students the central characters. **Secret Phrase** uses a fun mystery to highlight themes.

8 Rituals for Teaching and Training Online

01 Hand Shake Down
Get Shaking from the Start

02 Pass the Question
Spark a Constellation of Student Questions

03 Two Point Mashup
Support Student Remix Artistry

04 Hand Signal Expressions
Share Reactions and Requests While Keeping Flow

05 Pass the Mic
Give People the Stage

06 Previous Episode
Connect One Class Session to Another

07 Opening Credits
Make Students the Stars of the Story

08 Secret Phrase
Did You Catch That?

TOP-RIGHT HAND SHAKE

TOP-LEFT HAND SHAKE

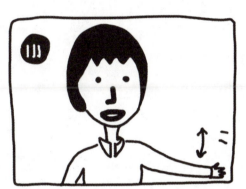

BOTTOM-RIGHT HAND SHAKE

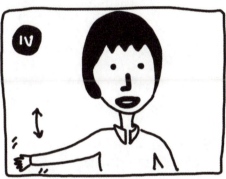

BOTTOM-LEFT HAND SHAKE

FIRST PUMPS IN THE CENTER

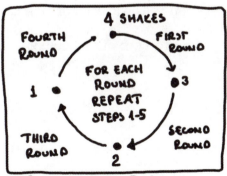

DESCENDING REPEAT

01 Hand Shake Down

Moment
At the start of a class.

This is a ritual that will work in **small and large groups.**

Intention
Get students loosened up and energized.

Time & Effort
Flies by! Takes 1–2 minutes.

What is the ritual?

You could just start class and jump into the material you want to cover. Or … you can get everyone energized with a short, fun physical warmup that students can do in front of their computers, wherever they are.

Four corners and fist pumps, let's go!

Backstory

This ritual is a variation of one the favorite stokes at the Stanford d.school, the Shake Down, which involves moving your arms, legs, and whole body. Those bigger motions can be a little trickier in front of a computer, especially if a student is in a tighter space at home and/or wearing corded headphones. So we tweak the motions to make it more accessible while keeping it fun.

How it works

1. The person leading the activity announces, "Okay, we're going to do the Hand Shake Down! You'll need to move around a little, make sure you don't have any drinks within arm's length that you might accidentally knock down."

2. "There are five motions in this exercise."
   - "The first is to put your right hand in the top corner of your Zoom screen, like this."
   - "The second is to put your left hand in the top corner of your Zoom screen, like this."
   - "The third is right hand in bottom corner, like this."
   - "The fourth is left hand in bottom corner, like this."
   - "The fifth is fist pumps in the center of the screen, like this."

3. "We're going to start with repeating each motion four times, then three, then two, then one."

4. "Ready? Let's go! [Right hand top] 1, 2, 3, 4. [Left hand top] 1, 2, 3, 4 ... (etc.)"

02 Pass the Question

Moment
During a class discussion.

This is a **small group ritual.**

Intention
Have students get their classmates involved in the discussion.

Time & Effort
Introducing and priming people can be under 5 minutes. The actual practice doesn't require extra time.

What is the ritual?

If we are not careful, virtual classes can end up revolving too much around the instructor. The class becomes like the solar system, where the instructor is the sun, and the students are the planets.

That's one model for a virtual class, but what if had a different metaphor? What if a class was more like a constellation and the students were the stars connecting with each other?

Pass the Question fosters a constellation dynamic. Instead of the instructor calling on students during a class discussion, students call on each other and get the whole class involved.

Backstory

Glenn is a huge fan of questionologist Warren Berger, author of *A More Beautiful Question* (Berger, 2016). Warren speaks about different ways to encourage more questioning in the classroom, including making questioning safe, cool, fun, rewarding, and sticky (i.e. make it a habit). Glenn created this ritual and hopes to one day ask Warren some questions about it. :)

How it works

1. This ritual is used during discussion portions of a class.

2. The instructor gives these instructions:
    - "I'm going to call on someone to pose an open-ended question to the class."
    - "After that person asks a question, they pick a classmate – one who hasn't yet spoken today – to share their thoughts on the question."
    - "After that person shares their thoughts, they call on another person who hasn't yet spoken to share their thoughts on the question."

3. "Keep going until I say, 'Let's start a new question. I'm going to call on _____ to pose it.' And then we repeat the process."

4. Depending on the flow of the conversation, the instructor might guide students to pose questions that build on a previous question.

03 Two Point Mashup

Moment
During class discussion.

This is a group ritual that can work both in **small and large groups.**

Intention
Invite students to synthesize different thoughts from their classmates.

Time & Effort
When first introducing the ritual, takes 2 minutes to explain. The mashup itself takes 2–3 minutes, and can spark a wider class discussion.

What is the ritual?

One of a teacher's most important jobs is to help students connect the dots, to tie together different concepts into broader themes and insights.

A teacher could that all herself. Or she could occasionally nudge her students to help connect the dots for their classmates.

Two Point Mashup is a ritual that challenges students to find patterns across different points that classmates have surfaced.

Backstory

One of the most important responsibilities of a teacher is to help students connect the dots, to synthesize different points into a cohesive whole.

However, that doesn't mean that the teacher should be doing all the synthesis herself or himself. One way we can help students to develop their synthesis skills is by nudging them to synthesize different points raised by their classmates.

How it Works

Here's an example with Juan, Lisa, and Marcus.

1. During a class discussion, the teacher says, "Okay, let's do a Two Point Mashup." The teacher then gives instructions like this:
    - "Juan and Lisa have brought up two interesting points."
    - "Marcus, try to put their two points together. When you combine them, what thought or question comes to mind?"
    - "If you'd like, you can ask Juan and Lisa some clarifying questions before you share your two point mashup."

2. Encourage and support the student creating the two point mashup.
    - If the student is having trouble formulating a two point mashup, ask them to think out loud and share what questions are coming to mind for them as they are trying to synthesize.

04 Hand Signal Expressions

Moment
Throughout class.

This ritual can be done in a **group of any size.**

Intention
Express a request or a reaction without interrupting the flow of a discussion or presentation.

Time & Effort
Takes 10 minutes to think through and test on your own. Takes about 2 minutes to introduce to the class. Then the signals can be used at any time.

What is the ritual?

In a virtual classroom, or any kind of virtual gathering, we want to help people to express themselves in various ways, including requests and reactions.

You could do this through chat, though many instructors can find it challenging to pay attention to what students are saying and what's going on in the chat.

Hand signals can be a great way for people to be able to express themselves in a way that others are more likely to be able to pick up on.

Backstory

Hand signals seem to have become more popular in classrooms in the last few years, but this ritual was particularly inspired by the resurgence of snapping at poetry events (Rosman, 2015). Snapping is an example of a spontaneous response that is noticeable but doesn't bring too much attention to itself and does not break the flow of the moment.

How it works

1. On your own, brainstorm what kinds of expressions might be helpful for your students to have available to them. Examples:
    *   Requests
        *   I have a question.
        *   I'd like to build on the previous point.
        *   I'd like to express a different point of view.
    *   Reactions:
        *   Applause.
        *   That was an a-ha for me (e.g. mind blown).
        *   Now I'm confused.
        *   I agree.
        *   I disagree.

2. Whittle down the list brainstormed in step 1 to the most important expressions. (It would be really hard to keep track of 50 different hand signals!)

3. Develop hand signals for each desired expression.

4. Test each hand signal in your videoconferencing program, to make sure that it can be clearly seen in Gallery View.
    *   One way to do this is to start a videoconference with just yourself, and resize the window to the size of what a single students looks like in Gallery View.

5. In class, introduce the hand signals to your students, so that they can use them.

6. You may need to periodically remind students about the hand signals as they get acclimated to them.

05 Pass the Mic

Moment
When you want to be extra careful of people talking over each other.

This ritual can be done in a **group of any size.**

Intention
Clearly give the person speaking the floor.

Time & Effort
Takes 1 minute to tell students how to prepare. Takes 1 minute to review the guidelines in class.

What is the ritual?

Sometimes in class discussion, we have the challenge that no one is saying anything. And other times, we can feel overwhelmed with many people wanting to say many things!

For the latter, it can help to have a ritual that provides additional cues of who has the floor to speak.

In Pass the Mic, each student has a physical object where they are seated that can be their "mic" – it can be a marker, a cooking utensil, a carrot, etc. Before someone speaks, they need the previous speaker to figuratively hand the mic to them.

Backstory

The logic of the Pass the Mic ritual is to provide an additional physical cue of who has the floor. This can help slow down turn taking in conversations so that people are less likely to speak over each other.

How it works

1. Before class, ask all your students to have a physical object that they can use as a pretend mic. It can be anything from a marker, a cooking utensil, a carrot, etc. Ask people to try to get something that is large enough to be visible on camera.

2. During a class, in a discussion where you'd like to use Pass the Mic, review the following guidelines with your class:
   - "We're going to use Pass the Mic for this next section."
   - "Remember, before you speak, you will need the person who last spoke to pass the mic to you."
   - "The previous speaker passes the mic by putting their mic down, and then the next speaker picks up their mic."

06 Previous Episode

Moment
Shown at the beginning of class.

This ritual can be done in a **group of any size**.

Intention
Connect the previous class session to the next session.

Time & Effort
You'll need to take notes of what your students say during class. Then 10 minutes between classes to prep. Then 2 minutes at the beginning of the next class to do the recap.

What is the ritual?

Imagine your course feeling more like a Netflix series, where each episode builds on the previous one.

One simple way to create that feeling in your class is the Previous Episode ritual. It's like creating that opening moment in a TV show where the narrator says in a deep voice: "In our previous episode ... "

You don't have to have that big narrator voice yourself. :) All you need to do is create a quick and simple series of slides with one line each, highlighting key points students explored in the previous class.

Backstory

In his essay "Previously On," television studies scholar Jason Mittell describes how an episode of a TV series can use a recap of the previous episode to cue the viewer's brain to move key information from slower storage in long-term memory to the faster processing (short-term) working memory (Mittell et al., 2010).

Glenn built on this insight, using the analogy of comparing class sessions of a course to episodes of a TV series, to create the Previous Episode ritual.

How it works

1. During a class session, take notes on key points and questions that your students raise.
   - If you can capture quotes, that's even better!
   - If you want to get fancy, also snap a few screenshots when students are making their points.

2. After that class session, and before the next class session, give yourself 10 minutes to put together a quick-and-dirty slide deck, a montage of key points made in class.
   - Each slide should have one line and person who made the point. Keep each slide concise.
   - Adding pictures of students in your slides makes it feel a lot more human! If you got fancy and captured screenshots, this is a good place to use them. Or you might have other photos of students you can use.
   - You can certainly include points that you, the instructor, made. But try to make the majority of it about what students said.

3. Open the next class session with the Previous Episode recap slide deck. (You're the narrator!) Try to keep this recap to 2 minutes or less. At the end of the recap, set up some suspense of what's coming next in today's episode ...

PRODUCTION
PRESENTS
THE COURSE
STARRING
LAILA ...
(ALL STUDENTS)
LET'S MAKE HISTORY

07 Opening Credits

Moment

At the first class session of a course.

This ritual can be done in a **group of any size.**

Intention

Make students the stars of their own learning story.

Time & Effort

For a simple version, you can put something together in 20 minutes. You can get a lot more elaborate with channeling your inner movie producer if you'd like.

What is the ritual?

Opening Credits helps students feel like they are entering a different world together, where they are the stars of the story.

Everyone's name appears on screen, either one by one or in small groups, with cinematic music playing in the background.

You don't need to be a professional video editor to create this! All this can be done in slide presentation software relatively quickly.

Backstory

When Glenn and Kelly Schmutte co-led the Stanford d.school's Summer Camp for Instructors in 2020, one of the most important things they wanted to do was to help build a sense of belonging, as there were many new instructors joining the teaching community. They opened Summer Camp with Opening Credits to show participants that they were the main characters in the story ahead.

How it works

You can use any slide presentation software to create Opening Credits. The explanation below uses Google Slides as an example. What follows looks like a lot of steps, but it can be quite quick.

1. Prepare your Opening Credits slide deck at least one day before your first class. :)

2. Get a list of the students in the course.

3. Create a new presentation in Google Slides. Choose a background color, font, and font color.
   - Example: black background color, "permanent marker" font, and cyan font color.

4. Do some quick math, as you'll want to keep the deck to 30 total slides or less.
   - If you have 25 or fewer students, you can plan on having one slide per student.
   - If you have more than 25 students, you may need to have two or more student names per slide.

5. Create slides with your students' names on them, in 48 point or larger font. Vary the alignment (left, center, right) slide to slide for visual variety.

6. Add slide transitions between each student slide. This is the one time you can appropriately go crazy on slide transitions!

7. Then create opening slides. For example:
   - Slide 1: _____ Productions presents ...
   - Slide 2: [name of your course]
   - Slide 3: Starring:

8.   Then create a closing slide. (E.g. "The journey begins ... ," "Let's make history," etc.)

9.   Finally, add a soundtrack.
     *   Find some free music on the Internet (YouTube Audio Library is a good source).
     *   Upload your music track to your Google Drive.
     *   In Google Slides, go to your first slide and select Insert | Audio, and then select your music track. In Format Options, select Start playing "Automatically," and then check the boxes for "Hide icon when presenting" and "Loop audio," and uncheck the box for "Stop on slide change."

10. Do a test run of your Opening Credits slide deck from the beginning, and advance the slides every 3 seconds or so.

11. You're now ready to show Opening Credits at the start of your first class!

08 Secret Phrase

Moment

Hidden in at least three spots in a class session, revealed after class.

This ritual can be done in a **group of any size.**

Intention

Have fun with an inside joke / game that references what we're learning.

Time & Effort

Takes 2 minutes to think of a secret phrase you can use. We'd tell you how long it takes in class, but that's a secret! (Read on and you'll be able to figure it out.)

What is the ritual?

There's something that can be super fun about inside jokes. It's like you are in on a secret. In a way, it can make you feel kind of special ... especially if it's something you can laugh about.

Secret Phrase is a ritual that harnesses the power of inside jokes, with a lightness that prevents alienating people who don't get it.

There is a secret phrase hidden in each class session. It might be in what the teacher says, or it can be in written materials (e.g. in slide decks). It will appear at least three times during that class session. After class, students can guess what the secret phrase was.

Backstory

This ritual was inspired by CrashCourse's "Phrase of the Week" that John Green would hide within videos. (Glenn is a huge fan of CrashCourse World History.) Phrases were suggested by fans in the comments on YouTube and hidden by Green within a video. During the credits at the end of each episode, Green would let viewers know what the previous week's phrase was.

How it works

1. Before class, figure out what your Secret Phrase will be.
    You might base the phrase on a key point from that class session.
    Try not to make the phrase too obvious. The fun and the satisfaction comes from the challenge!

2. Make sure the phrase comes up at least three times during a class session, whether it's the instructor verbally saying it or it appearing in written materials such as slides.

3. At the end of class, invite people to guess what the phrase is.
    This can be done in chat, or you can invite students to verbally guess in the final minute of class.

Leticia Britos Cavagnaro

Co-Director, University Innovation Fellows Program and Adjunct Professor, d.school, Stanford University

Leticia Britos Cavagnaro is the co-director of the University Innovation Fellows, a program of the Hasso Plattner Institute of Design (d.school), which empowers students to be co-designers of their education, in collaboration with faculty and leaders at their schools. Leticia has been working with distributed teams and with fellows all over the world for years, so she is no newcomer to virtual collaboration.

Leticia fosters a "people before task" mindset with her teams, fellows, and students. She underlines that we cannot turn our emotions on and off, so we need to make it okay to bring and share our emotions to our everyday interactions.

Rituals Include and Involve

One theme we noticed in Leticia's work as an educator and a leader is her use of rituals to include and involve everyone in a group. Her teams intentionally design rituals toward this purpose.

What can this look like in practice? Leticia gave an example of how her team structured a recent check-in ritual at one of their meetings. One team member had just gotten back from his sister's wedding in India. Many people in the team would be interested in hearing about that experience in the team's check-in, but might there be a way to do that while engaging everyone actively? So instead of just asking that one team member, "How was your sister's wedding in India?" the check-in question for everyone on the team was, "Tell a story about the last wedding you attended." This allowed everyone to share a story.

Rituals for Reflection to Learn Together

In all the different classes that Leticia teaches at the Stanford d.school, her teaching teams always have very strong rituals. Some of the most prominent rituals are around promoting and structuring reflection in learning experiences.

Leticia's classes require students to move fast and dive into action, stretching everyone's creative muscles. But those action moments need to be paired with deceleration moments to stop, take stock, and reflect on what happened and what it means. What might be my next moves, and how am I going to approach things differently next time? Reflection rituals force people to reflect on how their identity has changed or how their understanding has changed or how something has clicked for them.

What Leticia believes is really important is to make the reflections in these rituals visible to everyone in the group, as this gets people to synthesize reflections from multiple people in different ways. (Sidenote: Depending on the subject matter, sometimes the names will be taken off the individual reflections.) For Leticia, the value of reflection rituals is not so much about the "what" of the reflection, but instead the ownership of the learning process. She believes in establishing reflection rituals that transfer the ownership of the learning experience to learners and democratize ownership of a joint learning process.

And Leticia believes that these rituals translate very well to a virtual context, which opens up more options. Students can formulate, share, and consider each other's reflections synchronously or asynchronously. Having different digital spaces available allows reflections to be referenced and built on over time.

Rituals as Balance

Leticia makes the point that rituals can enable the right mix of knowing and not knowing. They help people be okay with not knowing what exactly is going to happen because they provide some structure to lean on. For example, "I don't know what's going to happen in the class, but I know that we always end the class with a reflection and we start the next class with the synthesis of everyone's reflections." Leticia poetically refers to this as "the island of knowing in the sea of not knowing."

11
Rituals
for Social
Gatherings

When your meeting is more informal and less about getting work done, these rituals can make your online sessions more fun, profound, and lively.

"Keep smiling, keep shining
Knowing you can always count on me, for sure
That's what friends are for"
– Dionne Warwick

At the time this book was written, during the COVID-19 epidemic of 2020, virtual socializing was a bizarre experience that was often frustrating and occasionally delightful. (Glenn will never forget watching in San Francisco his then four-year old niece in Orlando blowing out candles that were on a cake at another uncle's house in Portland.)

We will be curious to see how history looks back at this period. Will it be the era when people fundamentally changed how they wanted to interact online, shifting from performative social media to more genuinely personal video calls? Or will it simply be the time that we didn't know what the heck we were doing? :)

For now, we offer the rituals in Chapter 11 as ways to help your social virtual gatherings to be more fun, profound, and energizing.

Fake Surprise Birthday gives us an alibi for celebrating each other more than once a year. **Different Question** prods us to change up our conversation toward new discoveries about each other … and ourselves. **Name Tag** gets us to "woooooo!" **Best Thing I Ate** makes us hungry for more. **Play & Live Day** has us organize a retreat of creative activities. **Because DJ** justifies your musical tastes. **That Thing We Do** creates that special moment when we first see each other. **Spread the Warmth** shares the love.

8 Rituals for Social Gatherings

01 Fake Surprise Birthday
It's Your Birthday Even When It Isn't

02 Different Question
Break Out of the Usual Small Talk

03 Name Tag
You're It – Woooooo!

04 Best Thing I Ate
Who Doesn't Like Talking About Food?

05 Play & Live Day
A Retreat with Avocados and Ballet Class

06 Because DJ
Song Requests That Cost a Word

07 That Thing We Do
Everytime We Meet, How You and I Greet

08 Spread the Warmth
Feel the Love and Pass It On

01 Fake Surprise Birthday

Moment
When you randomly want to celebrate a friend.

This ritual can be done in a **group of any size.**

Intention
Let someone know how much they are loved and appreciated.

Time & Effort
Takes 5–10 minutes to coordinate deceptive chicanery. And then however long you'd like to celebrate together (15–30 minutes recommended).

What is the ritual?

Birthdays are great for most people. It's the one day of the year that we're most likely to get different people from our life wishing us well, expressing their love and appreciation for who we are as a person.

What if we could hear this more than once a year?

While it sounds great to have a gathering other than your birthday where everyone will celebrate you, many people wouldn't show up to their own non-birthday celebration. ("Oh really, you guys don't need to do that.")

And that's why it needs to be … a surprise.

Backstory

During the first couple of months of the COVID-19 pandemic, Glenn noticed that of all the virtual social gatherings he went to, the ones that seemed to have the most resonance were birthday parties.

To be sure, there were better and worse birthday parties, but the one thing that all birthday parties had was a clear goal: celebrate the birthday celebrant.

Fake Surprise Birthday takes that clear goal dynamic and it applies it to non-birthday social gatherings.

How it works

1. Check with your friends to see who you might throw a Fake Surprise Birthday for. The less that the person is expecting it, the better!

2. Have one person schedule a time to catch up with that person virtually, under the guise that it will be a one-on-one catch-up.

3. 10 minutes before the scheduled time, have everyone show up in advance of the person to be celebrated.

4. When that person joins the call, shout "SURPRISE!!!" Use of party horns and New Year's noisemakers is encouraged. Consider having background music.

5. Then one by one, do a round of appreciations for the non-birthday person who is being celebrated.

   Variation 1: You can do Fake Surprise Birthday more spontaneously at any virtual social gathering. ("Hey Vicky, some of us were thinking about how awesome you are! We're going to celebrate now like it's your birthday …")

   Variation 2: Fake Surprise Birthday can also be prompted with a random cue. ("Hey Todd, who appears in the top right corner of your Gallery grid? We're doing Fake Surprise Birthday for that person right now!")

02 Different Question

Moment

When you want to learn something new about someone.

This is a **small group ritual.**

Intention

Deepen a personal connection.

Time & Effort

Takes 5–30 minutes to play,
depending on the size of the group.

What is the ritual?

A lot of our conversations are a lot of nothing, as we go into conversational autopilot:

"Hey. How's it going?"
"Pretty good. How are you?"
"Good."
"What's new?"
"Nothing much. And you?"
"Nothing much."

What if our social conversations could bring out something different and deeper? In the Different Question ritual, we challenge each other to ask questions that the person we're talking with has never answered before.

Backstory

The logic of Different Question is to break us out of our usual small talk patterns with a different set of constraints.

How it works

1. Ask people at a virtual social gathering if they would be open to playing a party game called "Different Question."

2. Explain the premise: Instead of the usual small talk, in Different Question, you'll be answering a question that you've never been asked before.

3. Designate the first person who will be asked a question – let's call them the questionee.

4. Someone asks the questionee a question. The questionee now has three possibilities:
    *   If the questionee has never answered that question before to anyone, they can choose to answer the question.
    *   Or the questionee can say, "I'd rather not answer that particular question. Please ask me a different question."
    *   Or if the questionee has answered that question before, they can say, "I've answered that question before to someone else. Please ask me a different question."

5. After the questionee answers a question, they become the questioner and ask someone else a different question.

03 Name Tag

Moment

At the beginning of a social gathering.

This works for groups that are **small enough to fit on a single screen.**

Intention

Warm up people to talk and listen.

Time & Effort

Takes 1 minute to give instructions and about 2–4 minutes to play.

What is the ritual?

When we first start a video call, especially a social video call, it can feel a little awkward.

Name Tag is a ritual that involves calling out people (literally), putting your hands in the air, and yelling out "Woooooo!"

It's a quick little warm-up game, and by the end people will likely be loosened up, and perhaps smiling a bit too. :)

Backstory

Glenn created Name Tag by remixing an in-person game that he had experienced. In that in-person game, which he learned from Carissa Carter, people stand in a circle, you verbally tag someone by saying their name, then everyone tries to physically tag (touch) that person before they can verbally tag someone else.

Glenn was not trying to recreate that game in virtual, but rather take inspiration from some of the dynamics that made that game fun (e.g. the verbal tagging and the physical motion).

How it works

1. Tell your group: "We'll play a game called 'Name Tag' to get everyone warmed up, loosened up, and into the flow."

2. Ask everyone to get set up: "Get into Gallery View, and unmute your mic because it's going to go fast."

3. Explain how it works:
   - The person who is "it" tags someone by saying their name out loud.
   - The person who is tagged "receives" the tag by raising both hands in the air and saying "Woooooo!"
   - Now that person is "it." They tag someone who hasn't yet been tagged, and we repeat the process until everyone has been tagged. (For smaller groups, you might say that everyone needs to be tagged two to three times before the game ends.)

4. Play Name Tag!

04 Best Thing I Ate

Moment

At a major milestone or the end of a project or event.

This is a **small group ritual,** but can be adapted for larger groups by sending people to breakout rooms of five or fewer people.

Intention

Express gratitude for each other.

Time & Effort

Takes 3–10 minutes, depending on the size of the group.

What is the ritual?

Who doesn't like food? And who doesn't like to talk about food?

When we are interacting virtually, we can't eat the same food together, but that doesn't mean we can't share our food experiences.

In Best Thing I Ate, we share stories of the best thing we ate since the last time we talked. Pictures and eating reenactments are encouraged.

Backstory

When you're trying to help young people around the world break the ice and get to know each other in cross-national, cross-cultural teams, what is the #1 most reliable topic?

Glenn does not have rigorous scientific evidence on this, but what his experiences strongly suggest is that the topic is food. Everyone around the world loves to share stories of food!

Remember how in Chapter 3 we said George Loewenstein compared curiosity to hunger? Sharing stories of food activates curiosity and hunger.

How it works

1. One person starts it off by directing this question to another person: "Hey, _____, what's the best thing you ate since the last time we talked?"

2. The person who was asked the question answers, sharing what they ate and their experience eating it.
    *   If you have pictures of the food, sharing pictures is encouraged.
    *   If you'd like, you can act out a reenactment of your eating experience.

3. Then the person who answered the question asks another person the question, "Hey, _____, what's the best thing you ate since the last time we talked?"

4. As people share stories of food, they might also share where you can go to get that food. Unless they're keeping it a secret. :)

YOGA

DESIGN FOR FLINTSTONES

HOW TO GROW AN AVOCADO TREE

BALLET 101

05 Play & Live Day

Moment
When teams need a retreat for rejuvenation and connection.

This is a **large group ritual**.

Intention
Connect through creative hands-on activities.

Time & Effort
It can be a high-level effort. A lower effort version is possible by constraining it to internal team members.

What is the ritual?

Play & Live Day is a virtual retreat that comes from ATöLYE, a creative co-working space and community in Istanbul. It was designed during COVID-19 times with the intention of refreshing people with creative hands-on activities and increasing the sense of belonging by "being together online."

Atilim and Ayse are the ATöLYE community and talent team leaders who designed Play & Live Day. They wanted to make people feel like they could be together even though they were stuck in their homes.

The one-day event featured sessions that were structured around five main themes: physical well-being, mental well-being, arts, design, and gastronomy. Sessions included "Design for Flintstones," "How to Grow an Avocado Tree at Home," "Closet Drama," "Ballet 101," and "The Art of Pasta Making."

Backstory

Retreats are where teams break their routine and go to a special location to refresh and connect with each other. COVID-19 hit when it was time for ATöLYE's annual retreat in 2020. The constraints gave them the idea of Play & Live Day, to extend the retreat to the wider community members around the world.

As a team, they had been pushing the idea of creative community-building activities for years. For instance, they used to have creative gym gatherings, where teams worked on things such as designing a bee-house. They reflected on what they had learned from their prior creative gym gatherings, and decided to design a virtual retreat with the same intention of activating people in creative hands-on activities.

They put out an open call to their community members, who work in creative industries. The session lineup was very diverse, from drawing to acting, cooking to dancing.

Among 20 sessions, there were a couple of them that got ovations from participants.

The most attended event of Play & Live Day was the "Zoom Night Club," which was a dance party ending the virtual retreat. Gulnaz Or, who was also the DJ of the Zoom Night Club, framed the event as follows: "Do you miss partying all night long? Is your body feeling forgotten? Are you too lazy to dance at home? You're at the right place: ZOOM NIGHT CLUB." The only directive: Allow your body to move exactly how it wants to move and leave the control to music.

In "Design for Flintstones," the session facilitator Aysen Kusoglu asked participants to play a role-play game of time travel: "Imagine that the Jetsons ended up going to the age of Flintstones. Participants need to design concepts for the Jetson family using Stone Age technology. At the end of the game, we will vote on which invention will receive the Bedrock Innovation Award and a surprise technology grant."

In "How to Grow an Avocado Tree at Home," Zeynep Boyan aimed to gather plant lovers. She started the session by exchanging tips on house plant care and growing new plants at home. As a part of it, she shared a great quarantine project: growing avocado trees at home.

How it works

1. Have an open call for people to be a session host with emphasis on well-being, creativity, gastronomy, and other topics that you find relevant for your teams.

2. Based on the number of responses, create a schedule of sessions. If there are a lot of sessions, consider creating parallel tracks.

3. Think through the setup of your video call for the retreat.
   - Define a central session room where you start and close the retreat.
   - Define breakout rooms for sessions, and remember to give session hosts facilitator capability.

4. Have at least one highlight session where you can invite an external person (e.g. an artist) to bring a fresh outside perspective.

06 Because DJ

Moment

When you want a social call to have background music.

This ritual can be done in a **group of any size.**

Intention

Invite people to request music for their mood.

Time & Effort

Takes 2 minutes for your "DJ" to prep and give instructions. DJ will be DJ-ing throughout the gathering.

What is the ritual?

Because DJ is a simple ritual to make background music on a virtual call a little more interactive.

You have one person as the DJ, playing music and sharing their sound, and then you invite others to submit song requests. But it's going to cost you one word. :)

Backstory

Back in his college days, Glenn was occasionally called on to pinch hit as a DJ at house parties. He wasn't particularly good at it, nor did he particularly enjoy doing it, but he will never forget the "song request experience" (i.e. people yelling at you). :) This ritual is an homage that can add a little lightheartedness to the request experience.

How it works

1. Designate one person who will be the DJ for your social virtual gathering.

2. The DJ shares their sound during the gathering. For example, in Zoom: a) click on Share Screen; b) at the top of the dialog box, click on the Advanced tab; then c) click on Music or Computer Sound Only.

3. The DJ also has a music service ready, and has music playing.

4. The DJ announces that she will take song requests through chat, but it's going to cost you one word. We ask that song requests come in this format:
    *   [song name] BECAUSE [your one word reason for requesting this song]

BREAKOUT ROOM I

BREAKOUT ROOM II

BREAKOUT ROOM III

BREAKOUT ROOM IV

07 That Thing We Do

Moment
As your friends join a social virtual gathering.

This ritual can be done in a **group of any size.**

Intention
Greet each other in a personal way.

Time & Effort
Takes 3–5 minutes to come up with something. And then 5–10 seconds to do That Thing We Do each time we meet up with each other.

What is the ritual?

You can think of That Thing We Do as a customized handshake or high-five. You and your friends create a way of greeting each other on a video call that involves some physical motions that you make up.

Backstory

Custom high-fives have existed for a long time, but this particular ritual was inspired by the "Handshake Teacher," Barry White Jr., a fifth-grade English teacher in Charlotte, North Carolina. Mr. White had intricate, personalized handshakes for every single one of this students, inspired by each student's personality. There's something about that ritual that made each student feel special.

How it works

1. On a social video gathering, ask your friends, "Hey, we should come up with some custom way that we greet each other, like, you know, That Thing We Do."

2. Make up That Thing We Do with your friends! You might draw inspiration from various high-fives, dance moves, patty cake, exaggerated facial expressions, camera angles, etc.

3. Do That Thing We Do at the start of virtual social gatherings with that group of friends.

08 Spread the Warmth

Moment
When you want to send warm energy to a people on a virtual call.

This ritual can be done in a **group of any size.**

Intention
Convey care and well-wishes.

Time & Effort
Takes 1 minute to do.

What is the ritual?

Spread the Warmth is an elegantly simple and sensory ritual to send good thoughts to people on a video call.

It involves rubbing your hands together to create warmth, and then turning your palms to the camera to share that warmth.

Backstory

Jane Dutton told us about this ritual, which she learned from Chris Murchison, who is a passionate advocate for positive workplace culture. When we talked to Chris Murchison, he told us that the original in-person version of this ritual comes from her friend Vanda Marlow's professor Angeles Arrien. She called it Pearl practice to honor and share the wisdom of each participant in a group.

How it works

1. Ask everyone to rub their hands together briskly, to the point where you are generating heat.

2. Then tell people at the count of three, put your warm palms toward the screen and share your warmth with everyone on the call.

   Variation: Instead of doing Spread the Warmth to everyone on a call, you may choose a particular person or subset of people on the call to give warmth to (e.g. to mark a special occasion).

Mario Roset

Co-Founder and CEO at Civic House

Mario Roset is a Latin American civic entrepreneur who is the CEO and co-founder of Civic House, a collaborative space focused on empowering civic innovation organizations in Latin America. Civic House's resident organizations include the largest fundraising platform for NGOs in Latin America, a coding bootcamp exclusively for women, and a platform that fosters collaboration and allyship between companies and social organizations in Latin America.

Mario creates through connection. He finds new ways to connect people, passions, ideas, and resources. Mario thinks of new technologies as tools for social inclusion and for strengthening practices that seek to generate transformations. And Mario often experiments with new possible rituals to facilitate and deepen connection. Here are three different ways in which rituals can emerge for Mario.

Rituals That Emerge from Questions

Sometimes, a ritual has an origin story in a question. One question that Mario has asked many people is: "Where did you have great conversations in your life?" He's gotten several different answers, but the one that kept coming up was "road trips." So Mario looked at it more and noticed some of the dynamics of a road trip. You're seated side-by-side and are primarily looking at the same thing (i.e. the road ahead), but you can still look over at the other person occasionally to see their reactions. Mario hypothesizes that this can create more confidence and less confrontation, and can help you to give more honest responses.

From this, Mario has experimented with various forms of road trip conversations. An earlier form was with a Burning Man–like community in Argentina that created a fake road trip art installation. The group found an auto body of an old Fiat 128 that people could sit in and created a set of "road lanes" coming into the car from the front with a set of programmed LED lights that changed depending on how much people pushed the gas pedal. More recently, when lockdown measures took place for COVID-19, Mario started an Internet radio show where he goes on a fake 1-hour road trip with his show guests, complete with road noise. (The Road Trip ritual in Chapter 7 was inspired by Mario's rituals.)

Rituals That Emerge Accidentally

Other times, a ritual can come about by accident. Sometimes there is no conscious intention in its genesis. One example of this from Mario is his musical voice messages. One day, Mario was creating a voice message for someone and he happened to have Spotify playing music in the background at the time. When he was reviewing his own message, Mario noticed how the feel of the message was changed with that music in the background – it was kind of cool! Mario started playing around with it more deliberately. Before long, one of us (Glenn) was delighted to receive a Mario voice message on WhatsApp with groovy music. It felt like a virtual gift of sorts.

Rituals That Emerge from Other Rituals

Finally, sometimes rituals spawn other rituals. Mario has an annual ritual with Glenn, that they call the We Should Do Something Together! ritual. In it, they brainstorm different possible international collaborations that they might want to try that year. Sometimes, that idea exchange leads to other rituals!

One year, Glenn mentioned an activity he learned from a co-facilitator (Kaveh Sadeghian) at an Amnesty USA event. The activity involved putting the famous "36 Questions to Fall in Love" onto business card–sized cards. Mario transformed this workshop exercise into a ritual he uses with strangers and colleagues to create a context for deeper conversations. Mario expanded the question set, made everything in Spanish, and carried around a stack of cards he could use spontaneously. Pre-COVID, if you were to run into Mario in a bar in Buenos Aires, he might hand you a card with a question like, "What percent of your best self are you right now?" Mario is thinking about how to transform this card ritual for a virtual context.

References

Adkins, Amy. January 13, 2016. "Employee Engagement in U.S. Stagnant in 2015." Gallup. https://news.gallup.com/poll/188144/employee-engagement-stagnant-2015.aspx

Berger, Warren. 2016. *A More Beautiful Question*. Bloomsbury.

Benedetto, Ida. Personal interview with Glenn and Kursat. May 25, 2020.

Choose Your Adventure Series, https://en.wikipedia.org/wiki/Choose_Your_Own_Adventure

Collins, Randall. 2004. *Interaction Ritual Chains*. Prince University Press.

Crash Course World History. https://www.youtube.com/playlist?list=PLBDA2E52FB1EF80C9

Dutton, Jane E., and Emily D. Heaphy. January 12, 2016. "We Learn More When We Learn Together." *Harvard Business Review*.

Dweck, Carol. 2007. *Mindset: The New Psychology of Success*. Ballantine Books.

Epley, Nicholas. April 16, 2014. "Be Mindwise: Perspective Taking vs. Perspective Getting." *Behavioral Scientist*.
https://behavioralscientist.org/be-mindwise-perspective-taking-vs-perspective-getting/

Evans-Pritchard, E. E. 1965. *Theories of Primitive Religion*. London: Oxford University Press.

Evers, Chia. April 22, 2020. "Festschrift for Mike Hawley." *MIT Medial Lab*.
https://www.media.mit.edu/videos/mike-hawley-fest-2020-04-21/

Field, Syd. 1994. Screenplay: The Foundations of Screenwriting. New York: Dell Pub. Co.

Gandhi, Rujuta. Feb 4, 2019. "How to Lead a Meeting People Want to Attend." Gallup Workplace. https://www.gallup.com/workplace/246314/lead-meeting-people-attend.aspx

Geertz, Clifford. 1973. *Interpretation of Cultures*. New York: Basic Books, Inc. Publishers.

Goff-Dupont, Sarah. May 22, 2020. "How to 'Leave the Office' When the Office Is Your Home." *Atlassian Work Life*.

https://www.atlassian.com/blog/productivity/shutdown-rituals-for-remote-workers

Goffman, Erving. 1963. *Behavior in Public Places: Notes on the Social Organization of Gatherings*. Free Press.

Halvorsen, H. G. 2018. *Reinforcements: How to Get People to Help You*. Harvard Business Review Press.

Handshake Teacher. https://www.youtube.com/watch?v=I0jgcyfC2r8

Holt-Lunstad, Julianne. 2018. "The Potential Public Health Relevance of Social Isolation and Loneliness: Prevalence, Epidemiology, and Risk Factors." *Public Policy & Aging Report*, Volume 27, Issue 4, 2017, 127–130. https://academic.oup.com/ppar/article/27/4/127/4782506

How to Open a Beer with Paper. 2009. CHOW Tip. Jan 15, 2009. https://youtu.be/00DWLkVLbd4

Kearney, Christine. 2020. "Italians Sing Patriotic Songs from Their Balconies during Coronavirus Lockdown." *The Guardian*. March 14, 2020. https://www.theguardian.com/world/2020/mar/14/italians-sing-patriotic-songs-from-their-balconies-during-coronavirus-lockdown

Klein, Ezra. 2020. Marshall McLuhan as Explained by Nicholas Carr. https://www.vox.com/podcasts/2020/7/1/21308153/the-ezra-klein-show-the-shallows-twitter-facebook-attention-deep-reading-thinking

Kost, Ryan. April 26, 2020. "Video Calling Was Cool during Coronavirus Early Days. Now Comes 'Zoom Fatigue.'" *San Francisco Chronicle*. http://www.sfchronicle.com/bayarea/article/Video-calling-was-cool-during-coronavirus-early-15226472.php

Krukowski, Damon. 2018. *The New Analog: Listening and Reconnecting in a Digital World*. The New Press.

Lasar, Matthew. "'Keep Mustache Out of the Opening': A History of Phone Etiquette." *Ars Technica*, August 9, 2010.

Lafrance, Adrienne. "How Telephone Etiquette Has Changed." *The Atlantic*, September 2, 2015. https://www.theatlantic.com/technology/archive/2015/09/how-telephone-etiquette-has-changed/403564/

Liebermann, Matthew. 2013. *Social: Why Our Brains Are Wired to Connect*. Crown.

Loehr, Jim, and Tony Schwartz. 2005. *The Power of Full Engagement: Managing Energy, Not Time, Is the Key to High Performance and Personal Renewal*. Simon and Schuster.

Loewenstein, G. 1994. "The Psychology of Curiosity: A Review and Reinterpretation." *Psychological Bulletin*, 116 (1), 75–98.

Malinowski, B. 1948. *Magic, Science, and Religion*. Garden City, New York: Doubleday.

McCollough, Gretchen. 2019. *Because Internet: Understanding the New Rules of Language*. Riverhead Books.

McRobbie, Linda Rodriguez. June 20, 2020. "The Failure of Memory and Unreality of Time in Lockdown." *The Boston Globe*. https://www.bostonglobe.com/2020/06/20/opinion/failure-memory-unreality-time-lockdown/

Miller, Greg. Sept 8, 2014. "Data From a Century of Cinema Reveals How Movies Have Evolved." *Wired*. https://www.wired.com/2014/09/cinema-is-evolving/

Mittell, Jason, "Previously On: Prime Time Serials and the Mechanics of Memory." *Intermediality and Storytelling*, Nov. 29, 2010, Volume 24, 78–98.

Murch, Walter. 2001. *In the Blink of an Eye: A Perspective on Film Editing*. Silman-James Press.

Murphy, Kate. April 29, 2020. "Why Zoom Is Terrible: There's a Reason Video Apps Make You Feel Awkward and Unfulfilled." *NY Times*. https://www.nytimes.com/2020/04/29/sunday-review/zoom-video-conference.html?action=click&module=Well&pgtype=Homepage&section=Opinion

Nau, Dana. 2000. "Rules for Games of Charades." https://www.cs.umd.edu/~nau/misc/charades.html#:~:text=Charades%20is%20a%20game%20of,phrase%20as%20quickly%20as%20possible.

Norman, Don. 2013. *The Design of Everyday Things*. Basic Books.

Noy, Lior. 2014. "The Mirror Game: A Natural Science Study of Togetherness." *Performance Studies in Motion: International Perspectives and Practices in the Twenty-First Century*. Bloombury.

Ozenc, Kursat, and Margaret Hagan. 2019. *Rituals for Work*. Wiley Press.

Parker, Priya. 2020. "Together Apart." Podcast by https://www.priyaparker.com/podcast

Petriglieri. Gianpiero. 2020. "How to Deal with Video Calls, Zoom Fatigue, and Remote Relationships." https://goop.com/wellness/mindfulness/zoom-fatigue/

Renken, Elena. "Most Americans Are Lonely, And Our Workplace Culture May Not Be Helping." *NPR Health News*. Jan 23, 2020. https://www.npr.org/sections/health-shots/2020/01/23/798676465/most-americans-are-lonely-and-our-workplace-culture-may-not-be-helping

Richmond, Lauren L., and Jeffrey M. Zacks. December 2017. "Constructing Experience: Event Models from Perception to Action." *Trends in Cognitive Sciences*, Volume 21, Issue 12, 962–980.

Rosenthal, Rob. Personal interview with Glenn. June 2, 2020.

Rosman, Katherine. Nov 21, 2015. "Why Snapping Is the New Clapping." *NY Times*. https://www.nytimes.com/2015/11/22/fashion/snapping-new-clapping.html

Sax, David. 2016. *The Revenge of Analog: Real Things and Why They Matter*. New York: PublicAffairs.

Schwartz, Tony, and Catherine McCarthy. Oct 2007. "Manage Your Energy Not Your Time." *Harvard Business Review*. https://hbr.org/2007/10/manage-your-energy-not-your-time

Stephens, John Paul. 2014. "Leading a Group Through Feeling: Teaching by the Movement of Learning." *The Physicality of Leadership: Gesture, Entanglement, Taboo, Possibilities Monographs in Leadership and Management*, Volume 6, 17–36.

Swallow, K. M., J. M. Zacks, and R. A. Abrams. 2009. "Event Boundaries in Perception Affect Memory Encoding and Updating." *Journal of Experimental Psychology*, 138 (2), 236–257. https://doi.org/10.1037/a0015631

Tabata, I., K. Nishimura, M. Kouzaki, et al. 1996. "Effects of Moderate-Intensity Endurance and High-Intensity Intermittent Training on Anaerobic Capacity and VO2 Max." *Med Sci Sports Exerc*. 1327–1330. doi:10.1097/00005768-199610000-00018

Turner Terence. 1991. " 'We Are Parrots,' 'Twins Are Birds': Play of Tropes as Operational Structure." *Beyond Metaphor: The Theory of Tropes in Anthropology*. Edited by James W. Fernandez. Stanford University Press.

Tversky, Barbara. 2019. *Mind in Motion*. Basic Books.

Vallance, David. Dec 19, 2019. "We build our work lives around time but doesn't energy make more sense?"
https://blog.dropbox.com/topics/work-culture/build-your-worklife-around-energy

von Alvensleben, Laila 2018. "Online Warm Ups & Energizers." MURAL Blog. Sept 24, 2018. https://www.mural.co/blog/online-warm-ups-energizers

Webster, Andrew. April 23, 2020. "Travis Scott's First Fortnite Concert Was Surreal and Spectacular." *The Verge*. https://www.theverge.com/2020/4/23/21233637/travis-scott-fortnite-concert-astronomical-live-report

Wong, Wing Lum. 2019. Singapore Public Service. "Trending: The Loneliness Issue." *Challenge*. https://www.psd.gov.sg/challenge/ideas/trends/trending-the-loneliness-issue

Winnicott, D. W. 1973. *The Child, the Family, and the Outside World*. Middlesex.

Yeginsu, Ceylan. 2018. "U.K. Appoints a Minister for Loneliness." *NY Times*. Jan 17, 2018. https://www.nytimes.com/2018/01/17/world/europe/uk-britain-loneliness.html

Zacks, Jeff. 2014. *Flicker: Your Brain on Movies*. Oxford University Press.

Zack, Jeff. Personal interview with Glenn and Kurat. May 20, 2020.

Zimmerman, Erik. Feb 7, 2012. "Jerked Around by the Magic Circle - Clearing the Air Ten Years Later." *Gamasutra*. https://www.gamasutra.com/view/feature/135063/jerked_around_by_the_magic_circle_.php?page=1

Acknowledgments

This book would not be possible without the help of our family, friends, colleagues, and communities.

A big thank you to the Stanford d.school for being a place that connects. Our teaching community gatherings made our collaboration possible. Thank you to the members of our teaching community, who inspired us to share our work more broadly.

We thank all the people we profiled: Jane Dutton, Jeff Zacks, Jesper Frøkjær Sørensen, J.P. Stephens, Joumana Mattar, Laila von Alvensleben, Leticia Britos Cavagnaro, Marica Rizzo, Mario Roset, and Nick Fortugno. Thank you for generously sharing your perspective on how to nurture human connection in our virtual interactions.

We thank all the experts, community builders, and designers that we talked to during our research phase and who contributed to the rituals: Adegboyega Mabogunje, Alundrah Sibanda, Amanda Quraishi, Angela Washko, Annette Ferrara, Arne Carlsen, Atilim Sahin, Ayse Yazgan, Barbara Tversky, Bree Groff, Casper T Kulie, Christina Troitino, Dilek Demiray, Faisal Almutar, Greg Walton, Guilherme Amado, Ida Benedetto, Jane Dutton, Jeff Zacks, Jesper Frøkjær Sørensen, Jim Kalbach, Jo Sundet, Joe Allen, Joumana Mattar, J.P. Stephens, Kemmon Guadeloupe, Laila von Alvensleben, Leticia Britos Cavagnaro, Lior Noy, Lisa Kay Solomon, Marica Rizzo, Marina Walker, Mario Roset, Mark Tippin, Maya Gebeily, Melvin Chibole, Natalie Sebanz, Nick Fortugno, Odmaa Byambasuren, Peggie Sweeney, Rob Rosenthal, Robert Goldstone, Shahid Khan, Susan Burrows, Takuo Fukudo, Tania Anaissie, and Weixian Pan.

We thank Arnel Fajardo, Margaret Hagan, and Tomio Geron for their generosity in bouncing ideas, reviewing our writing, and giving feedback during our writing journey.

We thank Margaret Hagan for her support with the profile illustrations.

We thank our designer colleague Tiffany Tam for her support with layout design.

We thank our colleagues and friends who gave us feedback on book titles early in the journey including Emily Tsiang, Gloria Chua, Jocelyn Ling Malan, Julie Felner, Kate Judson, Mashood Alam, and Susie Wise.

Kursat's Acknowledgments

Thank you Margaret and my children Kerem, Teoman, and Leyla.

Thank you Mom, Dad, Selcen, Hamide, Meryem, Reyyan, Ahmet, Mehmet, and Metin for your emotional support while writing and drawing the book.

Thank you to the Stanford d.school students who always inspire me with their openness and hard work.

Thank you to my collaborators who taught with me before, including Professor Bob Sutton, Professor Ted Matthews, Professor Kajal Khanna, Professor Joshua Robin Mcveigh-Schultz, Margaret Hagan, David Sirkin, Isabel Behncke, Defne Civelekoglu, and Professor Anne Mundell.

Thank you to my advisors at Carnegie Mellon who helped me define who I am now over the years: Professor Richard Buchanan, Professor John Zimmerman, Professor Jodi Forlizzi, and Professor Lorrie Cranor.

Glenn's Acknowledgments

Thank you Mom, Dad, Arnel, Edwin, Thao, Kathleen, Mellie, Dom, Edison, and Diana. My favorite virtual ritual moment during the writing of this book was our family gathering for Diana's birthday, when she blew out candles that were in Portland from where she was sitting in Orlando.

Thank you to all my d.school students, particularly Amp Kittayarak and Gloria Chua. Thank you for your curiosity and energy. Thank you for pushing each other and for pushing me to find our deeper wells of creativity.

Thank you to my d.school teaching teammates, including Kal Joffres, Deland Chan, Jim Kalbach, Margaret Hagan, Jett Virangkabutra, Lesley Ann Noel, Nadia Roumani, Zvika Krieger, John Rehm, Jocelyn Ling Malan, and Emily Tsiang. Sometimes teaching feels like sunlight, other times like water, and yet other times like, uh, fertilizer... but it always results in growth. :)

Thank you to the d.school Teaching + Learning Team: Carissa Carter, Kelly Schmutte, Megan Stariha, Milan Drake, and Seamus Harte for being my community for much of 2020. I'm grateful for the time I've gotten to spend with you.

Thank you to my social innovation colleagues and collaborators around the world over the years. Thank you to the people of the TechSoup Global Network, especially Lynn Van Housen, Mike Yeaton, Nick Eyre, and Rebecca Masisak. A special thanks to Agustina Calcagno, Mario Roset, Melvin Chibole, and Natasha Murigu – my virtual collaboration brain grew by leaps and bounds in our collaborations. Thank you to the young people of the Borderless Youth Justice Network, particularly the inaugural cohort of the Borderless Fellowship for Justice Innovation, for bringing your creativity to the pursuit of justice around the world.

Finally, a big thank you to all of my friends for the moral support. If you're wondering, "Is he talking about me?" Yes, I am talking about you. :) Special shoutouts to Cynthia Wong and Jen Low for taking a look at early ideas when I was in is-this-making-any-sense-at-all? mode.

Authors

Kürşat Özenç, PhD

Kürsat Özenç is a designer, educator, and author. He is a design director at SAP Labs Palo Alto. He teaches design at the Stanford d.school and leads the Ritual Design Lab, where he runs experiments with students and partner organizations on personal, team and human-robot rituals. His work on rituals has appeared in *The New York Times, The Atlantic, Fast Company, 99U,* and Canadian Public Radio. He published his first book *Rituals For Work* in 2019. He holds a PhD in Design from Carnegie Mellon University.

Glenn Fajardo

Glenn Fajardo is a Lecturer at the Stanford d.school and was the d.school's Distributed Learning Teaching Fellow in 2020. He has been a student of virtual collaboration since 2008, working with people and organizations across six continents engaged in social impact work. Glenn was formerly the Director of the Co-Design Practice at TechSoup, a global nonprofit, and is trained in nuclear engineering sciences and public policy.

Index